I May Not Know What I'm Talking About

But I'm Gonna Say It

Anyway

By

Tara Ratney

To order additional copies of this book, contact:
Xlibris
1-888-795-4274
www.Xlibris.com
Orders@Xlibris.com
588803

Contents

Men Issues

Men Issues Continued The Dating Game

Tell Me Why Do You Play the Way You Play

Black Men Issues Continued

The Problem with Men is Sex

Black Men Issues Continued

Why is being a black man such an issue for you

Understanding Why You Can't Continue

Gay Issues

AUTHOR'S V@ICE

After coming into my own at the age of 40, I have, over the past several years, been able to sit down and reflect. Something which in some ways has brought me to writing, with me desiring to tell stories that reflected not only my own personal experiences but others as well. Initially starting off with screenplays, I thought if people actually saw an illustration of the day to day journeys of life, a light bulb would go off in their heads, where they might not only see themselves in the characters that I've created but that of those involved as well; with them getting a better perspective of the other person's point of view. However what I found was when people did read my manuscripts, they only looked at them for the entertainment value they brought (something which was great from the standpoint that they did indeed enjoy them) and not the lessons I was trying to convey; which for me created a problem since that was the real purpose for writing it in the first place. Hence explaining my partial motivation in creating this drama of words properly titled what it is; where through it a lot of straight to the point observations and self-discovery tidbits are passed on. Though I consider myself fortunate to been blessed with great insight, at least that is what I have been told, I by no means consider myself an expert, with me quickly advising the reader to look at this text as a firestarter only; from which I hope will motivate the person to do some serious soul searching, something in turn causing them to talk to those who do have the proper credentials to assist them further in their quest to a more fulfilling life.

THANK U(S)

To Yah for speaking to me daily, helping me to garner words of wisdom to share, because as those who do believe know through you all blessing flow and what I hope one day to be to others *(a blessing that is)* with you saying well done my child, well done . . . .

INTRODUCTION

In the beginning . . . .
The start of where some
of our problems began

Changing Environment, how we are raised, preparing for relationships, and parents no longer being self-employed or having the opportunity to pass on workable skills to their offsprings

Education, being not as important during the formative years of our elders as it is now, allowed those desiring to marry right out **school** (*or even before, if they chose not to finish*) **the** ability to do so; giving way to a more family oriented and less promiscuous society. **Young** ladies were able to focused their attentions on becoming wives and mothers as well as acquiring other skills that contributed to the household such as canning, sewing, etc. that could be sold at the **market** (*and/or for the purpose of bartering goods and services with others in the community*). Young men would work with their fathers learning how to hunt, farm or whatever skills the father had that allowed them to become b**readwinners** (*see the working together part where then the nurturing presence of a father was more evident*), **so** by the time the young man and lady reached what was then considered a proper age for m**arrying** (*something which could easily be before 20*), **they** were, for the most part, ready to step into the roles of being husband and wife. And for those getting on their feet, staying with one of the partner's families created not only a great bond for all concerned but also allowed the two to further get on board by working with those particular elders. However because of the industrial revolution first taking fathers out the home **altogether,** leaving the primary raising of children to the mother, then the educational system coming into play in a much greater way with all kids being required to finish high school and **beyond** (*something attributing to marring* *much later)*, **as well as**, changes in **dating customs** (*where things like chaperones being no longer part of the picture)*, **created** not only a greater desire to have sex outside the union (*you know from raging hormones with nowhere to go*) but an opportunity to do so. Where back in the day it was more acceptable to get married at an earlier age, also less children out of wedlock occurrences, also less exposure to different sexual experiences, because usually a person's first love was the only one they shared this kind of intimate bond with. However now, under this new environment, bigger problems have been created, (*from society not providing the kind of educational tools that could've aided in giving our youth a better understanding of consequences (allowing them to see why they should keep themselves until a more appropriate time) with us instead choosing to just throw rules at them, something resulting in rebellion*) leaving us with what we have now, sexual foolishness; a situation that has been going on for the last 60 **years.** (*Side Note: the difference between the former (educational tools) and the latter (rules) is one has the ability to teach through dialog and illustration where the other doesn't; depending only on scare tactics as a way of getting the message across, and what I feel has failed misery based on the fact that once kids were able to get out from being under the supervision of their parents they chose to run amuck, ignoring all that was instilled; an outcome no doubt resulting from the lack of true examples of madness to heed to (with any indiscretions that did occur being swept under the rug) with things coming off as only hearsay. A circumstance that no one today can say with there being plenty to base things on.)* **At** one time it use to be men who looked at women as sexual objects, only seeing the women they date as something to jack off into until they were ready to settle down. Now with women being more open minded, they taking a similar stance, are doing the same thing as well, which was never the intention of sex; something that was meant to create life should've never been looked upon as just being casual. Marriage is a covenant between man, woman and Yah, the one who created it, for two to become one, loving and serving each other with all that comes from it (*meaning children*) being valued in the highest regard. However over the past hundred years society has torn apart every institution for its own selfish purposes though sometimes understandable because of the letdown people have witnessed when they saw what they thought was truth turning out to being nothing more than a sham, with them in turn blaming the institution itself instead of the people living the farce causing them to rebel altogether. Along with delayed marriage, the break down of the family, with the removal of one or both parents from the home, where now there is a lack of bonding on the home front, hence one of the factors responsible in causing the sexual revolution.

Effects of a Changing Environment, the industrial revolution

With the industrial revolution again the father's presence was removed from the home creating the start of the breakdown of the family. Because we spend at least 10-12 hours away at work (*including to and from travel time*) there is only 4-5 hours, outside of sleep, left in the day for most parents (*namely the man*) to bond with their children and between activities, household duties, and downtime, that time is reduced down to even less. If the mother is a stay at home mom, she's the one who ends up carrying the load as it relates to child rearing so the child sees her as the primary caretaker thereby giving her more influence. If distractions come into play, such as relationship issues, work, outside interests, etc., it becomes easy for the man to detach and pull away from the family unit because he really has no vested emotional interest in it in the first place. And if both parents work, with the woman still handling the primary domestic duties, she may be putting herself in the position of spreading herself too thin, which causes greater stress on the family itself, again possibly causing her, him or both to look outside for comfort. Even if both parties work, with them making an effort to do things together (*something that would be considered the ideal situation*), the relationship is still vulnerable because of certain conditions such as when employment demands get in the way causing one of the parties to still have to carry the bill solo; which still could possibly cause resentment, again causing one or both parties to look for comfort from outside factors such as affairs, alcohol, drugs, and now even the internet. (*Side note: With most individual entities (like farms, small enterprises, etc.) no longer being left from big business swallowing them up the ability for our men to be captains of their ship has pretty much sailed when compared to what previously existed a hundred years or so ago; something that reduces him down to being just another pawn in those now holding the cards game. And because of this with the likelihood of him having very little say (or voice) could effect how he views himself where now feelings of inadequacy become part of his make up and what can eventually become a problem for those who depend on him, namely his family. So as women we have to learn to tread lightly, because when we don't with us looking to him for strength we may inadvertently overlook his needing to be built back up and what can cause him to look elsewhere if he doesn't find solace at home.*)

Sexual foolishness and delayed marriage, puberty didn't stop because we decided to focus on other things

Because society as a whole no longer looks at sexual relationships as just for married folks but for all regardless who it is with, we've reduced the act to just an act and ourselves to nothing more than a nothing, in some cases a means to an end, which was never Yah's intention. Woman was created for man because Yah wanted man to have relatable companion; something that complimented him that's why we are called woman because of us coming from man with it taking the joining of two again becoming **one**. (*Side note to women: When you man hate, you are hating on what comprises a part of who you are, think about it. Something also giving credence as to why homosexuality is wrong with us spitting in Yah's face from choosing what was never meant for us over what was.*) **While** man had no idea what he needed, Yah did and because of this he gave man great desire for woman, a sexual desire strong enough to motivate him to not want to be alone. Unfortunately however because of women knowing this use this information as a weapon, sometimes which again causes more problems as it relates to our relationships and the breaking down of them. And because men now feel they don't have to commit to anything to have sex, they treat women as only sexual objects using whatever come on they can to get what they want without any regard to feelings or consequence; again none of which was Yah's intention for what sex is for. Again sex creates life and should only be granted to people who are fully committed to each other without regard to their own **individual** interest or desires. If you are not in the correct mindset for that kind of concept you don't have the right to get married therefore sexual relationships are off limits to you. Coming to my next point about delayed sexual activity, as a society who gave kids in school the idea that they had rights when it comes to sexual relationships. Again, back in the day, it was common for young people to get married before the age of 20, but at the same time these same young people were also prepared (*or in the process of being prepared*) to take on family responsibilities; however once child labor and educational issues came into play, kids were encouraged to stay kids for as long as they can which means none of them are being taught life skills which again also means they're not ready yet to properly take on obligations pertaining to domestication; making sexual involvement asinine because what happens when they get together and become intimate, even if pregnancy doesn't come out of it, just plain foolishness and now with the rise of STDs occurring over the past several years amongst this group at a much more alarming rate, a lot of these kids are being exposed to lifelong health issues before they reach adult age and depending on the circumstances are creating an even more greater burden on society as a whole. Understanding the importance of a well rounded social background, the need for male and female interaction is definitely essential with non contact NOT being an option between the two. But question, um what happened to casual friendships I mean wouldn't it have been more beneficial if these young people learned to get to know each other as just people first before introducing the idea of romantic concepts with them looking at each other only in that way until they are in a better position to do otherwise. If you consider the practicality of this you will understand what I'm saying here. First you remove the idea of kids looking at each other as just a means to an end, because of friendship layers of depth could be added to a person instead of the two only seeing each other as to what they can get out of the situation, such as sex, financial gain, status, etc. bringing about sensitivity, consideration and more importantly respect; when a young man sees the young lady only as a sexual object she is reduced down to a nothing. Even if he loves her, because sex is attached to love, there is still the possibility of her being treated like an object. Just like when a young lady looks at the young man for financial gain or status, she too can in turn use her body or a baby as a way of getting what she wants which in turn causes him again to look at her as an object because he is looked upon as being only a resource and the vicious cycle continues. All the complaints we have about each other started at this critical age because of the many different experiences that have occurred during this time so as a society if we want more harmonious families we need our young people to have a better outlook than what they have not only seen but experienced. As far as preparation goes, there isn't anymore because of latchkey kids, baby having babies (*with the girl's mother usually taking on the role of raising the child*), the general focus on just academics in the school system and the removal of life skill classes such as home ed., vocational classes such as wood shop, carpentry, etc. as well as other social life skills programs have left them unprepared; even the elimination of programs such as art, music, etc., things that allowed young people who have talent in those areas to function without a formal education, have hindered them. And now since everybody has to do something else beyond H.S., something not everyone can afford, to make somewhat of a decent living for themselves as individuals makes again focusing on romantic relationships at that age just plain stupid. Causal friendship should be the way to go. No parent should be responsible for paying for their child's romantic activities. No young man, who has interest in that department, should be dating anything until he is properly prepared to take on the responsibilities of adult life; with him deciding later as to whom he should start focusing his romantic interests on and the same goes for the young lady. I have a daughter and trying to pay for her new outfit or getting her hair done for the fly guy who may not last but for a minute is not the business. I didn't start dating until I was on my own; so whatever dramas I incurred was not only my business but I spared my parents the financial burden of maintaining it; which brings me to another point concerning these years, one needs to find out what they like in a person first; when you're just friends you're not obligated to anyone therefore you're not restricted to one person. By getting to know different people without several issues being part of it, you get to see them again as a whole person without your judgment being clouded thereby avoiding hurt feelings because you didn't take advantage of anybody and more importantly you get to find out more about yourself;

which is what you need to do before picking out a mate; if you don't have a clear understanding of who you are, you will go from person to person, changing like the wind once you decide to move in another direction. As human beings we tend to lean toward people who are on the same page as we are. But when there is no certainty, we can find ourselves fleeing when we realize this is not the direction we want to continue in or stay miserable inflicting pain on ourselves as well as others, which is not fair to anybody and again why it is important that all of us need to understand the importance of commitment and the consequences if you don't, and MOST young people don't which is why they need to work on themselves first instead of worrying about romantic inclinations at this age. Another point not brought up earlier that definitely needs to be addressed is the fact that because most young people are still under the thumb of their parents, their true self has not yet been established, and what I mean by this is since most of us carry our children financially until they are able to stand on their own two feet, as well as, having major influence on the way in which they conduct themselves, what most of their peers are seeing is based on our dime and values, not theirs. And until they are fully out on their own anyone romantically interested in that person has no real ideal as to what they are getting if they date them before that time which again could possibly mean disappointment if he or she turns out to be a dud as far as how they handle responsibility, image, etc. A lot of kids base their decisions on who they associate with on popularity, not realizing that what they see now is not always what they are going to get later; the ones who appeared to be all that before adulthood, may, in the future, be broke, busted, and disgusted once they become adults just like the ones everybody wrote off as going no where fast turning out into being the pleasantly surprised successes. Which all says never judge a book by its cover until all the facts have come in and again why dating at this age may not be best during those years.

A suggestion concerning how we as a society might go about correcting some of the ills progress created, with my solution utilizing tools already in existence but in a more comprehensive way. Something I call a true and total life skills program starting at 7th grade with it going all the way through high school; a mandatory program where seniors, upon completion, would be required to pass a test showing reasonable comprehension of knowledge learned in order to graduate. Referencing parental, religious and secular points of view, the layout of this kind of program would encompass:

> 7th grade—sexuality and how to deal with it
>
> 8-9th grade—man/woman issues, self-esteem, platonic friendships, abuse (*mental, physical, and sexual, something if currently already going on in the home, counseling and possible intervention (with social and/or family services being brought in) could be included*), dating, committed romantic relationships, marriage, the effects of children in and out of marriage, child rearing, divorce, bullying, racial/cultural/class problems (*with students getting all sides of the story where now things like history can come into play in a much greater way*), conflict resolution, issues dealing with the law and its long term consequences
>
> 10th grade—the introduction of life skill classes beginning with education, as far as, preparing for life after high school where now in depth discussions concerning what

impact certain factors such as dating, romantic relationships (*heartbreak, long distance relationships, the managing of family responsibilities while in college/and or trade school*) and unplanned pregnancies can have on future plans during this time. Also, for the sake of giving a true visual, making available opportunities for students to take planned trips to different colleges as well as other post education programs

11th grade—all things career with again the subject of relationships being included in the discussion as it relates to the balancing of personal life with professional

12th grade—finance, with students learning about banking (*investment, saving, and checking*) credit, housing contracts (*with them understanding what they will be responsible for*) financial obligations (*household expenses, creation of personal budgets (from the standpoint of both single dwellers as well as family (whether it be as a single parent or married with children) based on different income scenarios (because after all not all of them are going to be ball'ers), etc.*), information on different outreach programs (*when additional assistance would be needed*), and final review.

Now along with open discussions and role playing there could be speakers (*medical and mental health personnel, ministers, financial and employment counselors, legal and college advisors*) as well as, theater groups (*or a touring company consisting of graduating theater/production students recruited from various colleges as part of a community service program where here through the use of plays and/or skits, further illustration of certain subjects can now come alive; with there also being the creation of DVDs to be handed out to students and/or libraries for all to review or even sold to the general public with the proceeds going back to the program*) brought in for additional reference. From all of this, I'm sure poses the question, Why in school and not an as extracurricular program? With my answer being why not since in my opinion formal education serves not only as an institution for learning but for social development as well (*with there also being a better overseeing as to what is taught*). And by giving our kids a different point of view as well as a surer footing certain patterns of behavior could possibly be broken, creating a commonality for all, thereby allowing for a better transitioning into a now social oriented world. (*Side note: As a progressive society it becomes important to consider consequences before ever moving forward with us first incorporating a plan of action on how things should be carried out because if we don't, with us choosing to ignore ills already inherited, will garner us a much greater burden to bear later. Example: Old problem—babies having babies; something due to changing values, New problem—displacement of workers no longer needed due to advancements made in technology. An additional side note: Concerning the above suggestion, there are countries in Africa that actually have schools that teach women how to be wives, something all saying that what I am proposing is not entirely that farfetched. Now for pro-lifers, with your agenda being to protect unborn children, why doesn't organizations such as yours promote more pregnancy prevention (with you having a building right next to Planned Parenthood, something definitely creating a choice), as well as, other programs that relate to proper family preparation, job training and placement (where child care options would be made available), etc.; things that might deter young women from choosing abortion, instead of just protesting, with my feeling being that talk without true solutions is cheap.)*

Reader's Notes

Chapter One

Women and the Games we play

I am not bowlegged

Lovers only see away I can't be

As they stepped to me with only images of their fantasies

At first, I insist then contradict my honesty

by hiding under camouflages of distractions and agreeing

with these obscenities

I'm not bowlegged

But by playing the game I'm furthered incriminated

and therefore carry the shame

Allowing myself to be reinvented

is there no one else to blame

I ask, can't they see the real me

Why do I fear rejection will come so easily

I'm not bowlegged

And knowing now what I need,

that is to be what Yah has made me

But first I must learn to love myself unconditionally

Then maybe others will see the limitations they set

before me, maybe then acceptances and respect will

become part of my destiny

Get it together girl, your desperation is showing . . . .

Being a woman and understanding our natural desire to be paired up is a little more than valid because that is what we were created for. However, the method in which we go about accomplishing this has done us more harm than we will ever know. Why we don't understand a man's hesitation as to why he doesn't want to be committed is beyond stupidity. The biggest pet peeve I have with us is what makes you think anybody who has the ability to come and go as he pleases, spend his money as his wishes, hang out with his boys as much as he likes, and not have to be responsible for anybody else would want to give that up for SOMETIMES sex, responsibilities of a family, including you wanting to stay home and depend on him as your primary financial source while you still want the nice home, social life, kids going to the best schools, etc. and not want to run for the hills. Ladies please I am a woman and would run. Unless he completely ADORES you and understands what it takes to make you happy, with him having no qualms about doing it, you can expect nothing but problems. And what is so sad about this is that we actually think we are selling him a good idea. I mean, life is hard enough just being responsible for yourself but when others come into play that can be more than a notion. Which is why we need to let him grow up; there is just no other choice, if you want that ideal relationship and I don't mean what we see in the movies or on TV, but the kind where the couple is thankful they made it to fifty years without killing each other and still find humor in it all, you have to be realistic because there will be ups and downs, trials and tribulations and we both need to be prepared for that, things do change; people go through stuff; and yes shit happens; it's all part of life in general. I just wish we would stop being in such a great rush to get there without making sure EVERYBODY is on board with this. I titled this section "Women and the Games We Play" because I know the great lengths we go through to get to the finish line. I've tried it myself and thank Yah, he put a stop to the madness, because the person I was trying to do this with, though he was my ideal guy, who I felt would have made a great mate and father, was not the one for me. And I had to, not without a fight of course, eventually respect his decision to move on because it would have been a terrible mistake to have gotten my way, doing what I tried not to do with my daughter's father which was to set a bad example for her by showing her what a sorry relationship looks like; poisoning her mind later with her hating men in general or doing the same stupid thing thereby probably living an even more miserable life. Coming from two different perspectives, one on my mother's side where the women are not too fond of men feeling for the most part that they are pretty much useless; with the women on my father's side feeling that they are nothing without one. Both set bad examples and depending on my mood I could go either way. For the first half of my adult life I allowed myself to believe that I had to be what a man wanted me to be for things to work out well I'm still alone so you see where that got me. And now with me being older I've gone in a completely different direction. Fortunately for me though I realize the part I played in my failures which keeps me in check when that evil twin comes out and I'm in that I don't give a crap mindset. But it is still there waiting to unleash on some poor unsuspecting man whose only purpose maybe is to just love me for myself if I'd give him a chance. Which brings to what I want to say to ALL WOMEN that it is time to let go and let Yah. Let him work on your dysfunctions instead of looking for a man to solve your problems, treating him like he's the end all when he's really not. Learn to love yourself and find your true purpose then once you do, you will be a better person for someone else. We all have a special assignment Yah wants us to carry out. For some it maybe to be just a wife and mother, which for those there is a man who wants to take care of you in the right way, of course, and will find you when he's ready to take on that venture. Then there are those who are good at multi-tasking, with you being able to handle the demands of a job and still have a family; for you there will be someone happy to work with you as you both take on the task of domestication together and lastly there are some of us who don't have a real desire to have a family at all and believe it or not there is platonic companionship out there for you too as well! Don't live the life society places on you just because that's the way they see it. Mothers should not impose on their daughters or sons, for that matter, to give them grandchildren. Yah gave you children to love and nurture so make the best of the situation by doing just that. When your children leave the nest and you still feel a need to be a mother there are plenty of opportunities to gravitate toward; teachers, counselors, daycare providers etc., being a foster parent or mentorship opportunities are also available to you or maybe you have a neglected husband who now may need your attention; so stop pressuring your children to do something that they may not even be ready for causing them to put pressure on somebody else who in turn may not be ready either, thereby again, making all concerned unhappy. If you read your bible throughout history the male population was always targeted because of fear of threat. Men are the first to go during upheavals (*as well as from things like occupational hazards and personal conflicts*) because they were and sometimes are still looked upon as being so important that if there are too many in one particular group the other group fears their existence which means that some of us are going to come up short when it comes to finding a mate and since bigamy, man sharing, women on women action are all frowned upon we should learn being comfortable with living a life without the romantic company of a man; notice I said romantic companionship; friends can always play an important part in our lives which makes the whole concept of attached people not having opposite sex friends asinine as well, I mean if you can't trust your partner then why are you with them. That should be one of the reasons you choose to share your life, love and body with this person because of good **character**. (*Side note: As people when we see someone we like, lust takes over blinding us to things we should be concentrating on, like good character, you know—dependability, etc. No one should be allowing superficial stuff to get in the way of commonsense. If the person can't pay a bill, show up on time for anything, show respect toward women in general, and I'm not just talking about the one he's currently involved with either, then he is not marriage material. Whatever bad character traits he has while you are dating him is only going to get worst if you marry him so stop trying to get married to this possible train wreck and if you did, take responsibility for not seeing the whole picture, whining to everybody else about him; nobody, except haters,* want to hear it; because most likely they saw them for the person they were, but in your desperation to be attached you didn't want to hear it. My best advice to women who are married to lames is to pray that Yah will either help you work through your problems or that he gives you a way out, like with the fool completely messing up so you don't have to stay. But again because of our need to be paired up, we play a lot of games, sometimes the kind that can be detrimental to others, namely the children you have created with this person causing greater problems. Remember children are a blessing from Yah, with him giving us the ability to create life so the world can benefit from the gifts they bring. And when we don't provide the proper environment for that to happen it is going to be on our heads, all again saying why everybody involved needs to be on the same page. Being with someone who doesn't think enough of you to commit to you is not an example of someone who is on the same page. Even if the person feels that he loves you, because he is not in the position to do the right thing, is putting all concerned in a bad place. Real men know they should be in the position to take responsibility for their actions, little boys don't; leaving the family, walking out when they knew they were in over their heads but because of lust, insecurity, selfishness, egotism, etc. they perpetrated knowing that they would not be able to come through and that things are more than what they bargained for. On the other hand, we too have sometimes backed our men into a corner with us challenging their manhood if they didn't make us drop it like it's hot, then when a child comes out of it, we place guilt on them when they remind us that (TONY) "The other night y'all" was our idea in the first place by telling him what a decent man would do under the same circumstances. This is where I have to pray because of my feelings on this cause again like I said earlier it's hard enough for a person to be responsible for themselves so to back that person into a corner by *putting them in the position of having to be responsible for another life on PURPOSE just ain't right! That's why I tell any woman I talk to that if I had a son, you would have one cold mother to deal with if I thought that's how you rolled. What I tell my daughter is just like I love you, somebody loves him and just like I would go down for you, somebody, on his behalf, might do the same, so don't put me in the position of tussling because of your stupidity, because after I finish with them, you're next.)* **Being** in a committed relationship takes a lot of work and both parties need to be mature enough for that. If the person you are infatuated with is not there right now doesn't mean it won't happen eventually, but that maybe it could be not only for his sake but yours as well with there still being things you need to do or work on allowing you to become a more complete person; something we sometimes forget. Again in our rush to get paired up we don't realize that the problem may not be him but us. All of us come from different situations that may not have been the best place and without finding out if we are on the right track we may continue behavior that needs to be corrected because that's what we're use to which is why we need Yah in our lives to help us become what we are suppose to be. One of the reasons I understand why things didn't work out for me when I was younger was because of my thought processes not being right; knowing what I know now I wouldn't have wanted a relationship in that way. I see the problems others have incurred from them getting into relationships in the wrong way and they are not happy; the insecurity, frustration, hurt they endure is not what I know represents a real marriage and not what I see Yah wanting us to have. Even though we live in an imperfect world because of sin, there is still something better awaiting to bringing things back together again. Our parents weren't perfect neither were theirs, consequently bringing about the passing down of a lot of bad influence from generation to generation and we have accepted it because that is all what we saw. But once you allow Yah to show you the light, as well as understanding where he should be in your life, he will work on you to not only know better but to do better. When you lower your standards you are short changing yourself as well as saying that Yah can't make what he knows is better for you happen with you having to endure disappointment until you realize the mistake you've made; then after coming to terms with the fact that you can't fix the mess you have gotten yourself as well as others, who are now involved, into, you either turn to another person in the hopes of them bailing you out, or wise up and let Yah come back in, working things out for you and again helping you to understand that it starts with him. When looking for a mate Yah should be playing an important part in that process. He knows all and sees all so he knows who has what it takes to go through this journey of life with you.

> Fine doesn't cut it
> Money and status ain't all what it takes
> Sexual antics only last so long before it gets boring
> Sometimes even being decent won't make it

The person you disregard now might be the one Yah is working on for you but you don't know it yet, then when it happens, with things manifesting themselves before your eyes, you see how things start falling into place, with regards to problems and issues being worked out. I've seen that kind of relationship with other people and I look forward to it manifesting in my life as well and if it doesn't, because of the kind of world we live in now, I'm ok with that too because I still have a full life and that's what we should be striving for first before ever considering bringing someone else into our lives. Compromising just to have someone serves no one well, even the person you are compromising for because you could be blocking them from what Yah has for them which is selfish. Playing games with our children's father because things didn't work out, I'm saying this, especially to those who are not married, is wrong. It took two to make that child so if you didn't think enough of yourself to make sure that things were the way they were suppose to be from trying to hook a man any way you can then you need to get over yourself and try to make the best of that situation. The child is here because of two unconcerned people's actions not by their own doing; making them pay for your stupidity is inexcusable. If the man doesn't want to be part of the child's life then give that child twice the love. Stop looking for someone else to pick up the slack as if it were their doing. Some of us, under different circumstances, wouldn't have given that passed over guy the time of day because of the one we were chasing after, now we're looking for him to come to our rescue; and if you don't understand why that could lead to a resentful man then you need to get a clue; taking responsibility for your part in this may open things up for Yah to come in and work the situation out; whether it be with the child's father, somebody else, or you just going it alone, he will work it out. (*Side note: Because of our inability to see the unforeseen is why we suffer, with things that would've normally been considered blessings (children, love, careers, etc.) now turning into experiences to learn from, designed in helping us to get back on track again or at least we hope (that is if we do choose to learn from our mistakes instead of being bitter bugs about them, blaming everyone else without looking at our own actions and motives as a possible contributing factor) understanding that we can't just make something happen just because we desire it is imperative, especially without actually really knowing if this was something we're suppose to have in the first place.)*

Our progress, how's it working for you?

Over the past 40 years or so a lot of us (*meaning women*) have made many strides in our careers, education, home life, etc. However though that might have been the case, we still operate as if we are dependent on a man in the same way our grandmothers and great-grandmothers were when they were mostly housewives. During the women's lib era, while we were burning bras, no one took into consideration that though we won the right to map out our own paths we never factored into the plan as to how to deal with things once we chose to have it all. Our men, though grudgingly, gave us their blessings to be what we wanted to be but not without a cost because though the blessing was given they never said they wanted to pick up the slack on the home front, nor did they stop wanting to be the man of the house either which puts some of us in a dilemma causing us to either force issues by making them take on more of the household chores or continue having careers while still maintaining our homes which again puts a lot of stress on us. The former circumstance is what I call "The Oppressed Becoming the Oppressor", where the non dominant group takes on attributes similar to that of the dominant one thus creating a vicious cycle of tic for tat. Because there was no plan of action concerning what we were suppose to do once we had the right to pursue our personal goals, instead of just being housewives, things went into the trial and error mode, with women still having a hard time balancing both causing some of us to either go back to the ways of our predecessors, others opting to not having families at all or as again just mentioned us choosing to bully our men in submission with us acting worst than them. Bringing the point of what I want to say, if you are lucky enough to find someone who is willing to work with you it is a wonderful blessing; however if you don't, you can't just whip someone into submission and think that there won't be consequences. A lot of men still have traditional values and desire a stay at home wife especially if we are not required to take on any of the financial **burdens** (*for those in that position, it's like having your cake and eating it too if you're not holding up your end; you want the freedom to pursue your goals and equal treatment on the home front with him still footing the tab; not going to happen! At least not for too long anyway*). **Whether** we like it or not it cost to be the boss and money is usually what is used to pay for it; not household chores or nursing kids, cause even with the house kept cleaned and our kids being well maintained, still doesn't compare to the expense of keeping a roof over our heads, food in the refrigerator, and clothes on our backs; without finance we'd be homeless. Good housekeeping is esthetics, important, but nothing without financial maintenance. Men know it that's why they find ways out of helping us. As far as they're concerned it is our problem if we're stressed out, after all we wanted the career something, outside the home to make us more feel fulfilled. Most of them didn't sign up to do the household thing nor is it what they thought was going to occur that's why we need to think long and hard about who we get involved with and not assume that a man is going to be sensitive to our needs in that way just because he said I do. Again if you have that kind of a mate count your blessings but if you don't, don't think that bullying him is going to work for too long because there are plenty of men who can find someone else and who will do exactly what they want them to do, remember the 4 to 1 rule, for every one man out there, there are 4 women. No man really has a problem finding one, it is the type of women he's looking for which is our trump card and how we trump him. Whether it be looks, good game, or whatever we use to reel him in, that's our ticket to achieving our goals as far as getting him and again since we know this we use it to the fullest until we are no longer able to maintain it which again is where bullying comes in leading him to looking at the front door, affairs, withdraw from the marriage, sometimes emotionally, where he sinks into a whole nother world. All of this because we wanted to force issues with someone who didn't sign up for this. If we want balance in our lives (*and I'm talking to those who don't have helpmates*) we have to start taking a good look at our romantic choices and why we want what we want. Getting married is not just something to do or a check off on your list of accomplishments; there's a lot of commitment and sacrifice involved. If you desire to get married because of you wanting a family or companionship (*cause remember even under that circumstance, your presence is still required*) then that becomes your priority not your job, the benz, or keeping up with your girlfriends. If your priority is your career don't worry about that other stuff until you are prepared to accept full responsibility for what you may have to give up, which means being resentful is not an option from not being able to still live the carefree life you were living or going on all those wonderful exciting vacations you were use too because you want to be able to do those same things without regard to your current situation, again get your priorities in order by saving the money you're currently making while you're still single for the things you want in the future such as a nice home, retirement plan—things you know that are going to be important to you when you are no longer able to pursue your goals in the same manner you would've once been able to before starting a **family** (*with this also being something that especially applies to women who make more money than their husbands with them now having to learn how to live off of an income that is less than what they are use to*). **If** you have a man who can do those things for you put your money away for yourself or your future kids as far as college, weddings, etc. that way you won't have to impose on your now husband in such a way that forces him to have to pick up the slack for you because of you not knowing how to juggle the work/home thing successfully. I'm saying this because though I will always be a working woman, and would like a man who helps **out** (*side note: I have no problem helping out with the bills, so I'm not trying to have my cake and eat it too, however, because of guy's ego issues, they make it hard for sisters like me, a subject that will be discussed later*). **If** I get so desperate to have a husband and he happens not to be the kind I prefer, then I will have to accept him for who he is; again bullying him into submission is not an option. With marriage being such a big deal I want to minimize as many unforeseen problems that I can and if I was content being single all these years with me living my life as I please, he may have been too, so assuming that he is just going to bend because I want him too. Unless he hunted me down like a dog to get me; which in today's times is not usually the case. We are the ones who want and demand these relationships again men don't have to because they can get sex, kids, etc. without getting married; with women catering to them without a ring being on it and them still moving on with their lives when they are ready too without the complications of divorce. Because we have given them their cake, we are the major cause of our own demise from not having a plan when we were burning bras with things becoming more of an advantage for them than us. Nobody ever achieves the "having it all", at least not all at the same time. You may get the career but things change when people start coupling up. The same goes for men too, if you want to run around all the time, then you shouldn't get married that's why women get first dibs on the kids when the relationship ends and why you find out the hard way that it's cheaper to keep her because no one is sympathetic to you; with you being looked upon as a paycheck only because of you being seen as making very little emotional investment which is what your family didn't need, they needed you too. And why both parties need to get their priorities straight before they say I do. Even with men having the option to move on, starting over again is a hard thing to do. Understanding that certain things, such as looks and status, are never constant is a sign of maturity and knowing how to make the best of your situation can save your marriage. (*Side note: Since as women we now have opted to have the final say in our lives (when it comes to relationships and intimacy with us now being able to move away from situations that don't work for us) makes us a lot more liable than our predecessors were (something being based on traditions and customs with them choosing to accept society's stance on this), and in saying this that means we can no longer lay blame on men concerning certain outcomes because of the stakes not being as high now as they were then when were we playing a more subservient role. With things being just as much our fault as it is theirs with us also needing to correct our own behavior (or beliefs) first before worrying about someone else's.*)

Respect me please, the consequences of getting our hustle on

When women think that men are just going to respect them on the automatic, we have taken things for granted. Respect is earned through our actions and responses to different situations. When we look at men as just a financial provider or status symbol those desiring to further their goals will play the game using our stupidity to their advantage, for example if I get all hyped up over somebody because of what I think they can do for me financially he will, in turn (*once it becomes obvious that this is what it is actually about*) be able to use this information to justify his actions, as far as, mental or physical abuse, sexual favors, etc. goes because he knows as long as he continues doing what I want him to do I will take it. That's why you should never desire someone for these kinds of reasons; it's like you're prostituting yourself with you giving it up to the highest bidder. Just like in the same way if you date someone because of how they look, when you desire someone for this reason and the person becomes aware of it they lose respect for you because they know you either have low self-esteem and are trying to ride their jock or that you're superficial and will change like the wind; in both cases things are not always constant and most healthy minded people don't want to be treated like a piece of meat but instead to be desired for the inner person, a more lasting proposition. When you get involve with someone because of who they are as oppose to just what they bring to the table you help create a feeling of security, no one in their right mind invests in things that are not solid there's no peace in it only temporary gain. That's why when a person feels you are being superficial they make a decision to get the most out of the situation; so when they go down they don't feel short changed and since they know what you want they run with it without feeling guilty because now it becomes a business deal instead of a possible relationship; the only people who don't do this are people who have low self-esteem themselves and don't know their worth. With them being so thirsty for affection they willingly allow themselves to be used for the sake of keeping you around thereby giving you the upper hand which was the plan in the first place however again like anything else eventually all people come into their own realizing their self worth with them deciding to stop the madness, which in turn leaves us fighting to get things back to the way they were. Bringing me now to the "why it's hard to let a fool go" section.

Why people continue to be a pain when they have been clearly been given their walking papers

When men do it, it is usually physical abuse or stalking; for women, it's mental abuse, stalking, loss of finance threats, manipulation and the list goes on. When you allow someone to make a fool out of you, the now then victimizer sees their way in the door and whatever tactics that got them what they wanted to that point, they will continue to do but now on a much greater level for things to keep going their way that's why if you don't stop it in the very beginning you are opening up a whole can of worms you will regret later. When you know you are giving someone your best you have a right to be appreciated for your efforts. However because most of us see people from a lustful standpoint we (*the taker*) don't in the beginning look at a person in a loving, caring way but instead to get our individual needs met that's why they (*the giver*) have to make it clear that things are a two way street and not assume that the other person knows it. If you want to be in a relationship you have to act that way; giving men sex without commitment is ho'ng (*or in this case with you looking to gain something, tricking*) plain and simple. Unfortunately though because of naïve thinking (*with us looking at this as a way of achieving the goal we desire* (*whether it be love, security, etc.*)), women have been taught to negotiate relationships causing us to do what we have to do to get where we want to go which could be more than what we bargain for because of us not taking the time to check the story first (*from us not knowing what his agenda is either*). Men know how to play the game and again like I said earlier if he feels like he's being used for something he will in turn game it until he has the advantage with you doing all the **work** (*which is another reason why it doesn't pay to chase after a man because when you do you have taken responsibility of the relationship away from him; it was your idea to do whatever, it is your doing not his which is why he feels free to walk away when he is no longer interested. Saying again If you don't know first what you are working with you can end up with anything*). **But** in our desperation to get into a relationship we dismiss the signs going after him. And since most people really don't hide them they assume we didn't care. So when you finally wise up with you deciding to leave this ill-fated affair they are the one who feels betrayed, and why they can't let you go. In their mind you took them at face **value** (*with you allowing them to mistreat you; with it also being them desiring to continue to reap the benefits as well from knowing that nobody else is going to put up with their foolishness the way you have*) **all** this time so why are you tripping now, with anybody, on the outside, who opposes the situation looked upon as being the one who caused the change that's why alienation is part of the victimizer's strategy because they don't want anybody else's opinion in the mix outside of theirs; they want to be your Yah with them creating the kind of dependency that forces you to stay. Another example of this is when men, thinking they are saving a woman, as well as, looking for the ultimate ego boost, over kill on everything, always offering to come to our rescue without knowing if they're really being appreciated which, when not the case, will turn into using on our part. Then when they decide to move on we will do all we can to keep them even when we know we too really don't want them ourselves, because we like the stuff they bring, not them but their stuff which confuses them because they think we really want them causing them to stay in that bad place with them getting nothing in return and us continuing to benefit from their stuff, with it being all their fault no matter how treacherous we were because they allowed it in the first place.

We stay we pay, again the importance of taking responsibility

From all that I just mention one might ask how do you resolve situations like the ones talked about thus far. Again if you are single you need Yah's involvement in your choices. For whatever reason, we seem to leave him out of the equation when choosing potential mates as if just because we desire it makes it right. Again we desire things for different reasons with mostly sexual, emotional, or financial security being at the bottom of our motives; when we look to someone to fill a void, we sometimes put that person on a pedestal, even to the point of making them believe that they have more value than Yah with us thinking that this person can give us a better life; and because of this they are now put in the position of having to fix all our problems, which they can't from having the same limitations as we do. The only reason we have what we have is because Yah allowed us to have it and when he decides to change the game and you still look to that person as a vessel you are putting yourself behind the eight ball and will eventually be shot in the hole of disappointment. Nobody but nobody can be all or do all, we were not equipped for that and the only one who can is the one we choose to ignore especially after thinking we've found someone or situation that represents what we want not realizing that it was Yah who blessed us with it and not putting things in its proper perspective can cost us greatly, that's why we are constantly hurt, because instead of looking to Yah to help fill the void we need filled so we can become a whole person, allowing us to be put in the position of finding someone who compliments us, we find people who we think have something we don't have allowing them to dominant us thereby treating them like they are now our Yah and without them we think we will fall completely apart which is so far from the truth, it is ridiculous. Though we were made to depend on each other, we do have the capacity to make it on our own. It's just from our own insecurities that mislead us into thinking that we can't. Some of these thought processes come from our environment, how we were raised or not raised or of our own doing because of feelings of envy causing us to constantly compare ourselves to others, disregarding the gifts Yah gave us; that's why we need him to work on us first then after that happens, with us understanding what still needs to be worked on (*as we will always be works in progress*), we'll be ready for someone; and based on what we know concerning how we are suppose to be received, treatment, etc, our level of expectation will be valued with Yah opening our eyes to the one he knows will be right for us. As far as for staying in a relationship that's not workable you need to walk away unless you are married, you are not bound to this person so why waste time crying over spilled milk. Even if that person could be someone you could have a future with, obviously the time isn't right otherwise things would have fallen into place. I've seen relationships where though there were problems things still fell into place because both parties wanted this to work and because of the consideration they had for each other they were able to look at what was important and went on from there without a lot of fanfare. Something like that lets you know that Yah was involved because he brought people together who were READY to take on the task of being in a relationship. Now for people who are constantly at war with each other you may need to do some serious evaluating as to why you want to be coupled up in the first place, like I've been saying, both might need time apart to put things in its proper perspective and for those who are married all I can say is that you made your bed and, with the exception of adultery (or in cases of abandonment where spiritual conflicts between believers and non believers are at the root of things; Corinthians 7:12-16) have backed yourself into a corner. The only option you have is legal separation on the hope that whoever is at fault will have the ability to see the error of their ways and get some serious spiritual intervention with you also doing the same with the hope that you too will see the part you played in it and what you can do to not to continue creating the problem by being either an instigator or enabler (*something if you don't could result in history repeating itself all over again*). We all deserve to be treated with love and respect especially in a committed relationship and without it you will be taken advantage of. If you are in an abusive relationship and the person doesn't get the message that you will not tolerate him (*or her as it relates to men being on the receiving end of the abuse*) harming you, you have no other choice but to lock them up in **jail** (*or have them placed in a rehabilitation center where they, though in a restricted* *environment, would still be able to work and provide financial support for their family with all parties involved receiving counseling until a formal recommendation is given saying that there is true evidence of resolve with the victimizer being able to then resume their life unrestricted along with conditions requiring that they continue counseling (in order to prevents a relapse) with it also being if the person attempts to go back to their old ways they will be placed in a mental facility (something being based on the fact that since it is obvious that this person is unable to comprehend that what they are doing is wrong then this can no longer be looked upon as being just learned behavior (or perception) but some kind of mental imbalance that cannot be easily corrected through counseling and temporary removal from their environment). Now of course there really is no such place as it relates to the first option wit the idea again being based on the realization that first with prisons usually creating more problems than they actually fix (with most folks coming out worst than when they originally went in) why, in situations such as this, continue relying on it as a solution, secondly putting the person in the position of feeling freedom without feeling it with them realizing that though they're not incarcerated, with them still being able to somewhat function, they are still stripped of their freedom, something all being due to their ACTIONS, and by also putting conditions in place that they must adhere to in order to avoid the second option might truly deter them from wanting to continue working under this kind of thought process.)* **or** in the case of mental abuse again legal separation because they need to understand that this kind of behavior merits help and will not be tolerated. So if they want to spend the rest of their life behind bars or experience the loss of you (*while again still being financially obligated to you*) because of their continued actions instead of getting the proper help let it be their call. Separation is part of the solution, with continued prayer and counsel because without it change will not occur. A lot of women might not agree with what I'm saying here but remember I'm not telling someone to stay in the same house with a person who is a threat to your physical and emotional well being but it is not abandonment from spiritual conflicts or again a**dultery** (*though the possibility of it being part of these kinds of relationships is great because of the person having a feeling of invincibility once they know they can treat you in this manner; something if the case will definitely give you a way out*) **so** there is no valid reason for divorce. However you do need to remove yourself from this kind of environment until that person decides to pull themselves together, a lot of times these people are only repeating what they've seen growing up (*or in some cases what they were advised to do in order to keep the other person in line*) and the mistake that was made in those situations was there was no consequence to the abuser. As humans we do what we think works and when a man or woman grows up seeing bad behavior in their childhood they get the message on what they can do to someone else, that's why there has to be consequence. Taking actions such as pressing charges without reconsideration or in the case of mental abuse, leaving with you limiting that person's ability to dominate you sends a message to everybody that what that person is doing doesn't work because it brings about loss. Just like not letting that person stay in jail for their actions because of them saying that they've change when they really haven't, tells those who've witness the event that all they have to do is put on a good show as a way of getting out of the mess they have gotten themselves into with them continuing the abuse later; even guys who cheat on their wives have seen other men do it and because the women involved have put up with it, they feel it is something they can do as well. So not creating consequences for bad behavior doesn't help anyone. When you separate without divorce you are actually acknowledging your part in this and what I mean by this is in most cases the signs of abuse was always there but you continued the relationship giving that person permission to do as they please as far as their actions are concerned. Even if they did it to someone else (*without them feeling some kind of remorse for their actions*) with you not considering that they could do this to you, you have opened yourself up to trouble and that's the part you played in it. Which again like I said earlier is why they think they can treat you in this manner and in saying that you are also obligated to work things out with this person while they are getting **help** (*with you yourself also needing to address some of your own issues (whether it being due to naïve thinking, desperation, you trying to play savior or exploitation (with you just getting a thrill out of living dangerously from dealing with so called bad boys); now as it relates to the other person something else that needs to happen here before ever considering entering into a relationship with a person of this nature is verifying that they have actually taken steps to correct their behavior (like with the person having gone to counseling) with there also being a sense of apprehension on their part from them too desiring not to move so quickly into another relationship before making sure that they, themselves, are not asking for their own trouble by dealing with someone who too may be volatile*). **Adultery** and abandonment from spiritual conflict are the only real valid reasons for permanent separation everything else we are expected to work through. Divorce is a very difficult situation for all concerned especially when children are involved. No matter what kind of relationship you have with that other person, you are still both the parents of those children. A few of us have been fortunate enough to meet another person who is able to slip in and be that missing parent but even with this there is still a void left with that child having unresolved issues in regards to the unavailable parent causing them to operated dysfunctionally when they get into their own relationships that's why Yah hates divorce because of all the problems it causes; family, friends, etc. are affected by this. People are forced to take sides or cut off ties altogether because they don't want to offend anybody all of which is nothing but a big pain. My parents have been divorced since I was ten with my dad either getting married or engaged 3 to 4 times and with every new face we, his children, are expected to go with the flow which is difficult and in my opinion selfish on his part because he doesn't understand from his point of view that he is the one who pledge his love to this other person not us. My mother is and will always be my mother like he will always be my dad that's it; everybody else are just extras in the mix at least in my life. I am obligated to show respect but anything else is not my obligation however for the new person that's not ALWAYS how they see it with them expecting those connected to that parent to be under the same rules as they are. I see and hear about these things all the time with family and friends being caught in the middle of it all with the only persons benefiting from it being the ones who caused the problem. That's why again I say choose wisely so you are able to stay in the commitment you make. Believe it or not you two are not the only ones affected by your choices, others are too! That's why we all need to understand marriage is not only a covenant between two people but Yah and if you keep him in it and take responsibility for your part in conflicts, he will work things out, even couples who are considered ill fit have a chance to work the kinks out in their relationship if they bring him in. But it first starts with you, deciding that this is the bed you made when you became husband and wife.

Question to whomever is in this situation, why do we think that ignorance is bliss

Relating to what I talked about earlier concerning working out your issues before getting involved, don't we understand the importance of being a capable person, or handling our own affairs, and the effect on others if we are not! Meaning if you as a person can't adequately take on responsibilities that involve yourself how can you expect to be an adequate mate. When the person we depend on is no longer available for whatever reason and we don't have the ability to pick up where they left off we can set off a chain of events that can be catastrophic to ALL concerned. That's why as wives one of our purposes is to be a helpmeet, not just mothers and housewives, but his right hand when he needs it. Just taking care of the kids and home will not cut it when he is no longer there and whoever wants you to do that is setting you up for a fall. Again I have seen this happen where the man did not bring his wife in on certain issues, nor did he allow her to contribute to the household, leaving her and their young children with nothing. The fortunate part, in this particular situation, was that she was able to pick herself up and give herself and her children a decent life. But how many women not having a clue can do the same. Part of loving someone is looking out for their best interest, whether the man can do it or him allowing you to do it for yourself. Anyone resentfully of that is more concerned about themselves and their ego than the relationship which is a sign that future problems are ahead; and the person who desires to be treated in that way, not wanting, to know or take on adult responsibilities, is not someone who is mature enough to get married. Because someone not wanting to deal with these issues is acting like a child, not a woman, but a child who is only looking to be taken care of and not in the least bit interested in the welfare of others. Because whether they realize it or not when something happens to the man, they, now still needing to be taken care of, will find somebody else who may or may not live up to the expectations they need met, which in turn if they have children, with that now gone person, can leave them in a vulnerable spot. There are a lot of children who have been abused, abandoned, etc. because of the parent needing assistance, getting tangled up with someone who made them choose between them and their children with the parent usually choosing the former. Again as women, in our desperate need for whatever, make dangerous choices, even men when they are not adequate in whatever department they lack in can possibly choose women who could care less about their offsprings. Look at the story Cinderella, the girl's mother dies, and the father remarrying then dies, leaving her at the mercy of her greedy stepmother and children or the father who was a wimp when he was married to his first wife, repeating the same pattern of behavior with the new one, someone just as demanding, who could care less about anybody else but themselves making sure they get what they want from him; that's why they got with **him** (*something also explaining why baby momma drama comes into play where the first wife, wanting to protect her children's interest, creates havoc in her ex's life by continuing to rule the roast*); **the** same for women if a man feels our desperation he will treat us and whoever is connected to us as he sees fit because he knows we are not going anywhere. Some men deliberately choose women who are vulnerable for this purpose, because they need us to be dependent on them so they can do as they please. All this spells trouble especially to those such as children who are vulnerable to the drama. A lot of young men lose respect for their mothers for this reason because in their eyes she prostituting herself for a **man.** (*Hint: One of the reasons why some of our young men look at women as being bitches and whores is because of what they are seeing at home so the next time society in general attacks these same young men for their feelings please take into consideration the kind of environment they have grown up in.*) **That's** why again you should be able take care of yourself. Expect the unexpected and be ready to jump in and take over for the man when you have too. No decent man wants his family vulnerable to foolishness that's why he would not be threatened by your ability to handle yours, he knows nothing is promised so why be upset over a back up plan. (Side Note: *As it relates to what represents a good wife check out Proverbs 31:10-31, where here a clear vantage point on what mates are suppose to look like is given with us understanding that the opportunity to have our own was always there*)

Taking advantage of somebody else's assets for the purpose of self-gain

For whatever reason, why do we as women feel that just because the man can pay the bill means he can take on anything that comes his way. When in reality that may not be the case. Now what I mean by this is you make a decent living, then he comes along also making a decent living, with you two getting together. Ok so for the sake of argument let's say before coupling up you each were paying $1000 a month for rent. Now because he is in the picture you think you can get a house over $2500-3000 or more with him paying the household expenses after all he is the man and should be handling that, since you are paying a third, not half but a third of the mortgage, this also doesn't include vacations, times out, etc. which too he is expected to cover. Illustration below:

His Then Expenses	His Now Expenses
Mg. $1000	Mg. $3000-1000 = $2000
Hexp. $1000	$1500
Exps. $1000	$1500
Savs. $ 500	$ 500
$3500	$5500

Now from the example above, if I did my math correctly he has at least incurred an additional $2000 of debt which is 57% increase from what he had before you two got together (*I am deducting his household expenses when he was single*) and the only reason he has incurred this debt is because you feel that the blending of **incomes** (*which when looking at this illustration is not a true example of that since he really is carrying the load, without* *any real assistance from you*) **creates** the kind of circumstance that will allow this to occur and/or that you also are probably trying to keep up with the Jones, showing off that you got it like that not realizing the burden you have put on him. Then when things become difficult for him to manage he will now be accused of not being a man (*or the man he was while he was pursuing you*) because he can't provide for you the way you would like when in reality you were being unrealistic. Financial problems is one of the primary factors for causing major discord amongst couples and we are usually the source from which it comes. If you couldn't take on a 57% increase in debt what makes you think he can without it being a strain unless he's got it like that, which if he did you probably wouldn't have to work in the first place. And if you know your incomes are comparable to each other, he can't do more than you. What would be the problem in getting a mortgage of no more than what both your rental payments combined give or take a couple of hundred with him paying the major bills and you, outside of your own personal expenses, putting something aside for various recreational activities (*including that of the kids*) as far as vacations (*or general outings, etc. this way you are guaranteed to have a night on the town from time to time*) along with some kind of contribution to savings or nest egg then when a rise in income and debt reduction occurs you can consider at a later date to buy a nicer house if it is merited; again wouldn't that work out better. Because our eyes are bigger than our stomachs we usually don't consider outside factors such as loss of income, sickness, separation, or death when taking on major debt like this and when something like one of the mentioned above occurs, it creates upheaval; personally I wouldn't feel comfortable taking on a venture like this unless I knew I could cover it myself, even with his additional income because of me desiring some kind of safety net in case the unthinkable happens. I know it seems like I am dumping on the ladies a lot, but after all this section is called "Women and the Games We Play". Now speaking of burdens on our men, why do we feel that they have to save every person we are associated with. I mean It's bad enough he has to worry about you but does he also have to be concerned about your dead beat brother, your grown children who you should have raised already to stand on their own two feet; the sad sister or those always in your face with their hands out friends, etc. I know everybody needs help sometimes and those a little more than others; but whether you realize it or not the people you deal with who are always down on their luck reflect on the kind of judgment you have concerning the company you keep, saying that either you are a user trying to take advantage of people who, if they are putting up with this foolishness, don't have sense themselves or that you yourself also are one of those same kind of drama persons, cause like they say birds of a feather flock together; which again says very little about you. We are all put here to be a blessing to each other, there is no doubt about that, but there is a difference between someone fulfilling their Christian duty and someone who has now been turned into an enabler. You are not helping people by doing too much for them, especially if they have obvious abilities to help themselves; that's not real love when you handicap people and its certainly not love when you put that kind of burden on your mate. Again one of our jobs is to put as little stress on the people we love as possible; making sure they stay strong as well as being sensitive to them even if they insist on doing things they shouldn't, demonstrates that. I think men appreciate us more when we show them that we are protecting their interests. I think it motivates them to go the extra mile for us when they know where they stand in our lives so don't allow outside factors to create doubt in his mind. If he feels the investment he has made into the relationship already was something that he shouldn't have, because of him thinking that he might be getting used, in the long run the loss of him will probably occur.

Is it him or you, I mean after all he is your husband

In marriage it is required that we forsake others when we take our vows, along with cleaving, and all that both have to do to maintain things, so why then do we have such a hard time accepting all of our man. Another one of my pet peeves is when it comes to things being about us, we expect to be the utmost priority in his life, but when it comes to dealing with him and his issues, we pretty much are ready to kick him to the curve. We don't want to deal with his feelings; we expect him to be strong all the time; his aspiration, if he desires to grow in someway, we want him to play it safe so as not to disturb our own security; problems such as issues he has on the job that may affect his future, we tell him to suck it up and deal with it because again of concerns about our own security and for me I've personally been involved in situations where the man, not being able to be honest about where he is not currently at, opts to instead to put on airs due to being afraid of his woman. When you expect so much from him, don't you think it is only fair that he should be able to come to you with anything; giving him a caring ear, a warm embrace and encouraging word. I thought that was one of our jobs and for me personally if I couldn't talk to the person I'm intimately involved with about everything whether it be past or present, then he gets dropped immediately, that is part of the requirement in being in a relationship with me. I see little sense in making an investment in someone who can't accept the whole me especially if they expect complete devotion in return, that leaves me feeling loved on condition only knowing when something he doesn't want to deal with, now becoming a problem, I will be drop kicked by him with the quickness which for me doesn't bring about any type of security and the same goes for men that's why side women come into play because they need someone to talk too! Even though they have made an emotional investment in you they still need to get some things off their chest and if they can't do that with you they will find someone else who will listen. Then after you find out that this has happened you take no responsibility for your part in it by putting all the blame of betrayal on him even though you betrayed him first because of your inability to accept all that comprises **him.** (*Side note to all men out there: if you have a woman who wants to be that shoulder, don't take that opportunity away from her, because by doing so, you hinder the chance for greater intimacy to be achieved thereby also hindering your ability in appreciating her more.*) **Sometimes** I think when a man turns to another person instead of the one he's actually suppose to be turning to, he is showing his lack of respect for both parties because he views both as objects with him having no regard for either of their feelings. The woman you choose as your mate is suppose to be your support system not just a show piece, just like the other person is not suppose to be some kind of side woman you create an unfilled alliance with, it is selfish and stupid especially when the loss of your relationship occurs because of it then you blame someone that you knew you had no intention of going any further with, but them just being the backup person leaving them to feel guilty over something that you are really at fault for. Something relating to this, why do we blame the other woman for our man's infidelity, if I'm not mistaken didn't he make the commitment to you, a, didn't he vow to forsake others and doesn't he know the consequence of **adultery** (*something if he doesn't causes the blame to be laid on you from you not putting your foot down when you knew he was out there doing his thing (or another way of saying this is deal with it because that's how you made it*)) **isn't** he suppose to not want to hurt you in that way because of what you mean to him. Doesn't he know that he is someone you greatly appreciate and in your eyes he is the cat's meow (*something If not the case then maybe that's why he's cheating, with you knowing that you have left the door opened for someone else who does*). So unless he is under lock and key, you have to believe that all the above questions are the right answers and if they aren't then whenever reason that caused you to commit to someone who's lacking is the reason for you being there and your motivation for staying (*you know like again with you marrying him for his money with that being all there is that's holds things together*), so again deal with it because you didn't want good character but probably something that means nothing now compared to the humiliation you're now have to endure because of you shortchanging yourself in the first place. Under those circumstances you and your mate made the kind of commitment to each other that Yah was not part of so the responsibility of keeping it is yours. Yah will always be there to help you through your issues if you bring him in, no one else except you three are really needed here. However, if your man is not honorable enough to do what he is suppose to do cut your losses and move on. Blaming someone else as well as going after that person is a waste of time because the only thing you are doing is puffing up his ego and when he gets his chance he will probably do it again and with someone else; that's the consequence of handling things in this manner, always having to deal with the possibility of infidelity happening again, praying that it won't with you having to suffer through it because like the point has already been made, Yah doesn't require us to stay in a marriage when adultery has occurred so if you do it's on you. That's why when I hear women talk about the difficulties they have when faced with getting past a betrayal with them being unable to forgive their men, I look at them as if they were crazy; I mean if you decide to stay you have no other choice but to let it go, holding grudges is not going to make your relationship better but worst; all of which causes someone like me to wonder why they seem not to be able to move on and if maybe that's the reason why the betrayal occurred in the first place because of their own vindictive spirit. Going back over some previous points made earlier, bullying and manipulation are not actions that help relationships grow but what tears them apart. Everyone has limits on how much they are going to put up with and without understanding this, with us thinking because of his now betrayal, we feel that we have him and that he is just going to take the abuse (*which again accomplishes nothing except the continuation of a never ending cycle of foolishness*); forgiveness is an essential part of the healing process, nothing else good can happen without it. So if your intentions is to make someone else's life miserable think first about what you could be cheating yourself out of—a chance for happiness later once you have gotten past the pain; whether it be moving on with you finding someone new, or staying with the two of you doing all the right necessaries, such as getting counseling, etc. Either way it is better than taking the low road to bitterness something a lot of women do, from trying to secure what they fear they could lose by controlling their mates, using guilt and anger as their weapon of choice instead of turning the situation over to Yah in the first place. He, and not us, has the ultimate right to judge as well as deciding our fate. So again if the pain of the betrayal is too much to bare, let him handle it and move on. Another point that needs to be made concerning this particular subject is the trust issue. I listen to a lot of people who speak on this subject and what they feel as being considered the correct behavior for the attached when dealing with the opposite sex; which is generally, you shouldn't! From pastors to common folks that seems to be the general philosophy, which when I encounter these opinions, I'm always left with a pit in my stomach because of the feeling that says that maybe the direction of smoke is coming more from the source rather than the one they seem to be so insecure about; meaning a rat smells his own hole first. When people know what they are capable of they accuse others of the same thing even when it's not merited because they can't separate their own acts of crimes from others. I never trust people who are always pointing fingers; what I have seen in those kinds of situations is that the accuser is either doing what they are accusing the other person of doing or will be doing the minute their insecurities get the best of them because it was on their mind all the time. People who don't think like that have the capacity to be open to others because they are coming from an innocence place, to them there is nothing wrong with being friendly or having opposite sex friends (*because they see people as just people instead of sex objects only, something mentioned at the beginning of the text*) and that's why I'm so bothered by those who do; restricting others because of their own issues is something that could eventually lead to future problems, such as, causing the very thing they feared the most, a betrayal. Everyone has something they bring to the table of life so it becomes unavoidable that someone other than you will not see it as well that's why trying to keep a person under house arrest because of you trying to protect your interest is unrealistic, you have to trust that the person you are involved with understands boundaries and cares enough about you not to cross them. I'm sure as you read this, you are asking, "but what if the insecure person has been betrayed before and is just trying to protect themselves from it happening again or that this is what they were taught". Well under the former circumstance I would say that maybe the person hasn't gotten healed yet and shouldn't be getting involved with ANYBODY until they do; it's not fair to bring past garbage into a new relationship. Making someone else pay for another's betrayal will push them away and if the injured party finds themselves dating people who have similar value systems to that of the person who betrayed them, then it's time to start asking themselves why are they drawn to these kinds of people and that maybe some serious counseling needs to happen first before they jump back into the dating scene again. Now for the latter, I would highly recommend that these people look at the person's situation who is passing this information on, seeing where their relationship is and if they want to follow in the same footsteps of the one giving the advice because they may find out that they don't. A lot of times, when we have gone through things, our outlook becomes distorted causing us to think that everybody's situation is similar to ours. Remember trust issues are usually based on the following:

a. How you got him
b. Your state of affairs when you got him
c. Your motivation for wanting him
d. How you view the opposite sex

On the flip side of the above section, if I can't trust you when you are not in my face I certainly can't trust you when you are

Those of us, who because of being involved in unstable relationships, can find ourselves overcompensating by cutting ourselves off from others because of lack of self trust within oneself. Instead of facing problems head on, we try to pacify the situation with the hope that it will keep us in line when in reality we are only avoiding the inevitable. One example of this is where while listening to someone talk about how they couldn't wait to get home to their wife when they were away, they, in the company of other women, didn't want to be put in a compromising situation by associating with them too much so they immediately left, heading back to their room to spend the remainder of their trip by themselves. Now I know a lot of women would ask, what's wrong with that, he avoided a problem. But that's just it he avoided a problem which could lead me to believe that even though he may not have done anything, he probably wanted too, and that's problem. Upon hearing this, if I was his wife knowing that he went too such great lengths, would not put my mind at ease but again lead me to think that maybe he is at war with himself and that once the right/wrong opportunity presents itself he would run with it. Sometimes as women we, greatly hungering to feel secure in our relationships, have a difficult time distinguishing between true acts of devotion and that of desperation causing us to miss the signs that there could be trouble ahead in paradise. That's why checkpoints in ones relationship needs to occur to help keep couples from taking each other for granted and not doing so with continued issues festering beneath the surface can erupt into a betrayal. Going back to a previous point made earlier about questionable information being passed on to others, the above scenario could also be considered an example of just that because the speaker, when discussing the issue, was using this as an illustration as to what he thought EVERYBODY should be doing in similar situations, which to me would have been valid if ALL of us were in the same boat, (*or shall I say had the same problem he seemed to be having, because obviously he was having one*); when it comes to dealing with the opposite sex on a casual basis; something if not the case could result in one of the following happening:

a. you taking what is said with a grain of salt

b. quarantining yourself from people unnecessarily because of a feeling that you are doing something wrong by JUST BEING YOURSELF

c. your mate, because of them cosigning with the advisor, checking you because now they feel they have a valid reason to do so which in turn could lead to possible resentment because of their actions being based on someone else's issues rather than yours

Another problem that we as women have, concerning our relationships, is the letting of outside influences mess things up; ladies if it ain't broke don't fix it! If your man hasn't given you a reason to believe that he doesn't know how to conduct himself in the company of other women do not impose rules on him because of another's advice (*or your own insecurities*). Now as for those who have hemmed themselves in because of self doubt, again you need to be honest with yourself and possibly your mate as to why you feel that way. When you enter into a relationship you should have a clear understanding of what you want and be able to commit to it too the fullest, taking complete responsibility for your decision. That's why **the answers from the above highlighted (a-d) points before this section concerning trust issues** have to be right because if they aren't with things not being either on the up and up when you got into the relationship or you just getting into it for the wrong reasons can help create doubt as to if you should be in the relationship thereby making you vulnerable to temptation as well as causing your mate to feel insecure. And since the foundation of your relationship is shaky, acts of desperation could come into play. One of the reasons I am putting such great emphasize on trust and insecurity issues is because I think couples need to stop arguing over something that may be a nothing with them learning to choose their battles more carefully. Unnecessary restrictions can not only affect your relationship, but how you live your life; from your job to even how you relate to your family and friends. A pastor can't effectively serve his congregation, nor set a good example for others by showing that they, themselves, have self control, if they can't demonstrate it because of limitations put on by either himself or his mate. Your partner can't effectively do their job or expand their professional horizons, if they are required to keep themselves under lock and key; and as for family, are they suppose to be exclusive when it comes to social outings because of an in-laws rules. Example, there was a situation where a **family** friend came to a function the sister invited her to with the now married brother being afraid to greet the friend because of his wife; mind you, there was never any romantic involvement between the two, but because of the wife's insecurities an awkward moment was created. Or in another case where the man is unable to hang out with his sister, because of his wife feeling that it's improper for him to be alone in the company of other women outside of her. Stupidities like these contribute to some of the reasoning behind why most singles, namely men, are so discouraged about getting married. Who in their right mind would want to be bothered? And this is really the point of it all, it's time as people that we see things from not just our point of view but others as well, because it's costing us greatly when we don't; with a wedge being created between singles and attached people, where now the former become instigators instead of a support system and the latter living in fear of them because of it. (*Side note: With us having the ability to regulate ourselves (from Yah giving us free will), we as human beings shouldn't have a problem doing the same in regards to how we relate to each other; and with that being said placing reigns (as it relates to this topic, not general laws or rules that have been put into place for the betterment of the whole society) on another person is, in my opinion, unnatural, with it only showing how much we allow insecurity to cloud our judgment (something that leads us to taking things into our own hands, where because of unbelief (or lack of faith) we think we know better than Yah). Now of course the biggest problem with this is us standing in our own way. Remember Yah will only allow to happen what he feels needs to happen in order get us to where he knows we SHOULD be. So by not allowing life to take its course we could be cheating ourselves out of a more fulfilling destiny; with the question being what if you did allow life to just happen and what you feared the most never happened, with you now knowing the true extent of your mate's devotion from his demonstration of loyalty; something that you might've never gotten a chance to witness first hand yourself if you were still operating out of a fear of lost.*)

The Black perspective, loving each other ain't always so easy to do

Another issue that needs to be addressed is the Black experience and the effect it's had on how we relate to each other intimately. Though most couple relational-ship problems are universal across the board, added issues of slavery and Jim

Crow have hindered us as a people from achieving the same kind of blissfulness that other races enjoy. Being forced to make the best of circumstances during those times, has put us in the position of accepting behavior that would be considered unacceptable by everyone else. Understanding how these two catastrophic events destroyed our families, this never ending story continues to engulf us because even with things seemingly being better now than they were then, we still operate as if we are under the foot of them; everything from settling to perpetrating we've done it for the sake of having a piece of something. That's why we're in such a mess and until we raise the bar, as far as good character is concerned, that's where we will remain. Most of the issues discussed throughout this text applies directly to us. As a people, getting a clearer understanding on how things are suppose to be will help us move away from what shouldn't be. And again that's why it starts with Yah. Coming from a black woman, that last statement sounds kind of strange, because I know a lot of us feel that we do have a strong spiritual foundation. In appearance, yes but when we look at what's going on in our lives where is the evidence of it. Looking to those who them, themselves, were forced to deal with the hand that was dealt them, for guidance instead of seeking the truth is no longer viable. We are now in a time where we are ALL accountable for everything we do. It's evident in our children and their outlook on life; our men, and their lack of respect for us; and in us with our own cutthroat mentality doing whatever it takes to get where we have to go. Taking a stand for what's right is the only way we're going to see the light at the end of tunnel. So if that means your man walks out on you then let him, what's yours will come back and the way it SHOULD once Yah gets his hand on the situation. Choosing to allow Yah to help you through the storm instead of turning to using or compromising will not only inspire you but others to do the same, as well as, showing them who's really got our backs; and lastly become more aware of what you're putting out in the universe, because it will come back and sometimes in the form of what your offsprings will either be or bring home. With us mostly being the heads of house, raising our children alone, we're all they have, so setting a good example is very crucial. If your daughter sees you hustling men or being negative toward them she, in turn, could grow up doing the same thing or bending over backwards trying not too which could possibly cause her to become a victim herself. Just like how, as mentioned earlier, the way your son defines women in general having a lot to do with what he sees in you, something to think about when it comes to his potential mates along with how he may handle relationships. Something else pertaining to this subject is the fact that because we are the heads of our homes our daughters have natural mentors in us where as with our sons they don't so the importance of giving them good support systems is again **crucial** *(with the question being for me here is, with us being fully aware that a disparity exist, why are we still so concerned about the ones (our daughters) who already have a proper example at home (mothers, grandmothers, etc.); with it being if they are not, shouldn't we be mentoring them (the example) instead so they now will be able to serve all who are under their influence better. Something else relating to this issue here is if what's at home has a stronghold (or influence) over these kids with the person themselves lacking, all the outside mentorship in the world is not going to make much difference when it* *comes to changing that child's thought processes until those wanting to make a difference get to that parent first with the only other option being left, outside of this is completely removing the child from this kind of environment. Now the reason for me bringing either of these points up is because, as it relates to the latter, me witnessing first hand how those on the outside wanting to do their part failing miserably because they just couldn't get past the child's allegiance to their parents and as it relates to the former, with so much emphasis being put on girls now days, our boys always seem to be left out and with them seemingly being the ones who really do need positive role models wouldn't it make more sense to place the focus on getting them proper ones; where now they both would have equal footing. Besides if our daughters are doing great with our son's not then what exactly will be gained here cept that of a wider gap being created with women continuing to be put in the position of having to settle, just something to think about!*); **within** the family structure there should be a source of encouragement, daughters and sons should not be pitted against each other especially when the son is the odd man out, it could cause resentment as well as contributing to the breakdown of yours and his relationship. And by fostering a nurturing environment the probability of the two transferring these qualities to other situations is greater bringing about more loving and healthy alliances for both; with the daughter trading bossiness and intolerance in for understanding and the son, who would have otherwise felt a need to flex, becoming more sensitive, as well as protective. Additional issues of concern are: The Mammie" Syndrome—something where, because of the unpredictable ness of a man's presence in the home, women develop unhealthy dependence on their children causing not only problems with the father but hindrance when it comes to their children's continued social development as far as how they relate to the opposite sex. In some cases the only reason a woman would even create an alliance with a man is to have a baby with her having full intentions of discarding him later. Other circumstances that usually bring about this syndrome is abandonment on the man's part, with the mother not allowing his influence to come into play; or in cases when he is there, emotional withdraw resulting again with possible abandonment. This all coming about because of the removal of our men from the family during the years of slavery and Jim Crow; something which left a lot of women holding the bag when it came to the raising of children. And because a man's presence became less and less important the lowering of standards, as to who we get involve with, is now the norm with us either looking to our sons to play the surrogate man in our lives or not allowing them to grow up at all and in the case of our daughters, them having to deal with our constant interference into their relationships. Something else that has been going on lately is the "Breaking them down to make it" Syndrome where we, with the assistance (*or encouragement*) of our female elders, use the creation of a baby as a way of forcing our men into committing to us; something I'm seeing more and more of in our community. For most of society it is commonly believed that it is the young man, who pressures the girl into having sex, however with the increase, over the past few decades, of babies having babies a lot of our daughters, never knowing their fathers, grow up hungering a man's presence thereby now feeling the need to be the aggressor when it comes to intimacy; and with their mothers also never really having the opportunity of coming into their own themselves, they become the daughter's accomplice. All of this of course being to the dismay of the boy's family, who, and I am talking about the ones trying to keep their sons on the right path, find themselves at war with the girl and her people with the young man being caught in the middle because of him being raised to do the right thing; outcomes that usually occur from this situation are:

a. alienation from family, with the young man being force to choose
b. interruptions of future goals, because now the young man has to take on new responsibilities with usually no assistance from his parents, due to the occurrence of (a)
c. if resentment comes into play or the young man sides with his parents, baby momma drama or just outright abandonment
d. in some rare instances, based on the maturity of the girl, everybody gets over themselves with things eventually working out

All with the exception of d, serves no one well, particularity the child, who again is the real victim here, because regardless of the young lady and her family's motives, the young man involved was also aware of what was expected of him so he can't exactly be taken off the hook when he knew he was wrong and now you have people operating dysfunction ally with the child possibly growing up not seeing what a healthy, loving relationship is. Another point that makes this all a sad commentary is the lack of guidance the young lady truly has. She's in fact been encouraged to use sex as a way of achieving her goals, which is to hook a man anyway she can with both her and her mother benefiting because again usually in this kind of situation the mother herself is also in need. Most young men lured into this pool of foolishness, are what we call the good ones, with them either being the kind who have been taught to be respectful and responsible and/or have definite potential; that's why they are targeted. And because of the mother's own mistakes, she attempts to rectify them through her daughter by living through her not realizing that if this all turns out to be a bust, the daughter could end up in the exact same boat she's in. Something else to be said about all of this is that how again we as women miss the opportunity to not only encourage our men in a positive way but at the expense of our own shortsightedness stifle our growth as a person as well, something that needs to happen in order to break the cycle. Having a distorted focus causes us to put more emphasis on our own needs, through the demanding of all his time and resources; and by making everything about us, his ability to strive for what he should be striving for, such as, getting through school, career goals, etc. becomes almost impossible. Again we are here to be helpmeets not a weight of burdens to be pulled around his neck; allowing him to find his way in peace with us finding ours can bring about the kind of union where we walk together; which if meant to be, is the real objective; and if it's not we're still ok too because as we move forward, under the continued process of coming into our own, we prepare ourselves for what is. Potential doesn't validate the decision that this is a person you should be getting involve with, especially when he doesn't have all his ducks in a row yet; again understanding the importance of order and why it needs to be followed will help avoid drama and heartache in the future. Aggressive behavior, such as, chasing after or us even putting ourselves in the position (*you know like doing things for the sake of getting his attention*) of being chase by a man works more against black women because of limitations that racism and poverty have imposed on us as a people; with a lot of our men needing to play catch up. Not always having access to the same opportunities afforded everyone else retards our development as far as finding our place in the world thereby affecting a lot of our men's ability to settle down at a time when society thinks they should. Even for those who we consider to have made it, because of them being new to the game, their desire to find out what they've been missing prolongs their readiness to couple up permanently; and with us going after them the way we do, what reason would they have not to weigh their options since they know they've got us already. And that's the problem because we have made them the prize instead of them looking to us as being one with them now playing us like three dollar bills. And until a man discovers you, he will never value you or see you as someone he can have a future with. Now for those who we see as having potential unless he, from a long term standpoint, values your presence in his life, things will:

a. eventually fall apart as far as anything solid occurring goes
b. turn into drama with you having to find a way of keeping the relationship going until he decides to buckle in and accept things

c. if you have the upper hand, go your way as far as you getting him, with him giving up his aspirations and you being disappointed because of what you thought you were going to get you didn't get; which is almost the same as b except there he still pursues his goals while you put up with the crap

With order he will, find his place in life, become ready to share himself with someone, and then find you. Things have to go this way because if they don't, you could find yourself experiencing one of the above all because of ???? (you answer that). Remember relationships are something we naturally gravitate toward with us being created for the purpose of being in one where as for them they were not so it takes more than just our presence for them to take that leap and why we have to wait. Making this again another reason why we need to look at the part we play in our man's dilemma with us making sure that we're not contributing to or just out of sheer ignorance minimizing certain situations as if they weren't our problem. One of the missions of a racist society is to create internal conflict within our group so if we as women look at our men as failures then those who we consider to be our oppressors have succeeded. We will never have successful relationships if we are always at odds with each other. And allowing the very ones, who helped put us in the position of being an oppressed people *(remember they have the ability to map out their destiny as they please)*, to set the tone as to what should be going on in our homes is crazy. I know no one can completely use racism as an excuse for not taking responsibility for their own lives, but we do have to admit that there are challenges with regards to how the other side consistently finds ways of throwing monkey wrenches into the plan. I see it all the time, where the already qualified brother up for a promotion is passed over for the fresh off the street college boy or the one who had a good idea being either ignored or mocked; things like this create problems especially if we feel that he is not living up to our expectations. Forgetting that we still haven't exactly overcome, puts us in the position of being unrealistic; so unless you're one of those who believes in entrepreneurship with you assisting your man in with whatever endeavor he decides to pursue, you'll have to face the fact that he can only do what he can do. And by not doing so, you'll be fighting a losing battle when it comes to trying to keep up with the other team, as well as causing dissension in your home. In reference to us supporting our man's endeavors, we as a people have always had to reconcile with the issue of being "last hired, first fired" a fact we've both lived with and feared since entering into the mainstream employment market. So why then do we as black women in our quest to maintain or keep up not allow our men to invest into a backup plan just in case the rug is pulled out from under them or from the standpoint of making a difference create the kind of opportunities that not only may put them on the map but possibly benefit others in our community as well. Having what it takes to succeed is no guarantee when it comes to longevity in a ruthless world whose only concern is about bottom lines; making the whole idea that one can afford to just rest on ones laurels because of the thinking that they have arrived unwise and why as women, who truly desire security, need not for them to put all their eggs in one basket. But we do, even to the point at times of putting our men in the position of having to compromise for sake of continuing the status quo. Of course the real problem here is how we again miss the chance of not only encouraging them to be all they can be but of being part of their success through our assistance instead of just riding their jock because of it. Final points on this subject, goes back to something else mentioned earlier with regards to our young ladies and how they, being so self-absorb, motivate our young men in the wrong way, as well as them putting too much emphasis on romantic relationships instead of platonic ones. Because of where our men aren't versus where we are educationally, puts us somewhat in a dilemma with us being force to:

a. move on without them
b. step back with hopes that they will eventually appreciate the support by playing catch up
c. abandon our own ambitions all together deciding if we can't beat them join them
d. if doing this with strings attached, work with him, even at the risk of drama with either him moving on or you keeping him under lock and key because of you wanting to protect your interest, which could still lead to him bailing out anyway

All of the above is based on two factors: ones own self worth and the importance of a man's presence in our lives. None of which are true solutions because in someway or another loss would occur defeating the whole purpose as far as bringing us together. So how do we as a people, particularly women, go about making things right here? To me going back to where the problem began is where the solutions lies. When young men approach a certain age, usually between 10-17, they tend to lose interest in school and with many of them not having positive role models to count on they follow whatever's put before them which again is usually other men who have no direction either. On the other hand with our young ladies having plenty of positive examples to choose from, in the form of their mothers, other female elders, teacher, etc., they have a better foundation to work off of thereby giving them the encouragement they need to succeed. Now where things start taking a downturn for both is while our young ladies continue to strive, our young men, heading down the beaten path to no where, don't; and with them interacting with each other romantically issues begin to surface as to how to make things work; with him either hustling to make his way through (*something that could possibly lead him to going to jail*) or eventually pimping her (*causing her to abandon or delay her goals*). Again none of which are acceptable **outcomes**. (*Side note as it relates to the above points from (b) and (d): In rare cases (when the young man does take the initiative by bringing himself up to speed) situations such as this can work themselves out from the two being able to weather the storm of adversity with them both learning patience. The problem here though being is not that success is unobtainable but that the couple, themselves, is asking for unnecessary trouble; something occurring just for the sake of pacifying their own insecurities (or selfish desires; which in most cases is usually the true culprit), because between them getting from point a to point b there will be a few ruff patches along the way; now of course a lot of us would say when it comes to relationships things like this come with the territory, something no one with any kind of real sense would* *disagree with, however understanding that there is a difference between natural and unnatural adversity with the former being based on true unforeseen circumstances like health issues, loss (death and employment), or family obligations (with things being totally out of a person's control regardless of how things came together) and that of the latter with it being based on our decision to proceed with something prematurely when just waiting for a more opportune time would have garnered a much better result. Something a lot of us don't initially consider until things get tense or when regret decides to rear its ugly head with us wishing that we had done things differently.)* **And** this is where what I talked about earlier concerning learning to be friends first comes in. Instead of these two looking at each other romantically before either are prepared to deal with such issues, they could grow in friendship with the young lady encouraging the young man to be the best he can be without **strings attached** then once things start rolling for him that's when they could consider the possibility of taking it to the next level; and if things turn out not to go in that direction, it's still not a loss because of their now great friendship with him gaining a better outlook on women because of his crossing paths with someone who was more about the positive than her getting hers through him; also by seeing that she took the time lets him know that there's hope in finding a person who has a compassionate heart. However, the unfortunate part about these kinds of situations is that in most cases our young ladies reward the young men with sex for buying them the baby phat or for putting all their focus on them something the young man really wouldn't have time for if he was handling his business. Of course the other side to this is when the young lady, desiring his attention, forgoes her studies for the sake of maintaining a relationship if she involves herself with someone who's lacking; which again makes what I'm saying about her encouraging him in the right way an advantage for her as well because while he is working on himself she can continue doing what she was doing as far as her studies goes. A side note to mothers: If you are going to put your house up for the sake of saving your son, wouldn't it be a better investment if it was for the helping of him in pursuing a positive enterprise rather than just bailing him out of jail because of a negative one. Waiting until he gets into trouble before making some kind of effort is pointless because now the damage has already been done (*with you possibly having nothing left to work with once you, from doing this, have exhausted all your resources*), where as doing it while there's still a chance of keeping him on the straight and narrow, by nurturing his talents or passing on ideas that could, eventually lead him to finding his way. (*Additional add on, with reference to supporting our men and integrated relationships; when looking at who's actually under the heels of oppression (1, white women and other non black minorities, 2, black men, and 3, black women.) it's easy to see why black men and non black women would gravitate toward each other. And what I mean by this is with how society looks at black folks in general, crossing the other's path (with them (non black women) possibly being stalled) while reaching for the top would create an opportunity for commonality to occur; as black men would be looking up versus looking back. (With the only way that not happening is through better self worth where they not only see value in themselves (as well as us as we would be looked upon as a real asset instead of liability (something being the same for other women of other races as it relates to their own men where now they would no longer seek refuge in the arms of ours from feeling the other's pain)) but have a sincere desire to improve our race's current state of affairs where they would no longer be interested in following the paths of others. Now I know a lot of black women would argue that not only are we moving up the latter, but are even surpassing our men, which unfortunately is one of the issues and why I am bringing it up; with it being that instead of us walking together we're walking ahead of them ALONE as MOST (due to the very same racist philosophy (orchestrated by those (meaning white men) that put us in this position in the first place) have found no one else to latch onto.) Another previously mentioned point coming out of this is since there are those of us who really do work off of bad concepts (something we seem to have a hard time acknowledging), pushing them away will become a continued trend. Again not fully grasping the true impact of racism on this particular relationship is our major downfall and being why that should have been our priority first instead of worrying about gender issues initially.)*

The Black Experience Continued, I'm Your Mother, not your lover

Another subject that needs to be touched on before bringing all this to a close is what our sons see in us is not necessarily all what they should be getting in a mate with the same being visa versa. And what I mean by this is with you being his mother there are things allowed you, such as discipline, parental guidance, as well as care. But when your son only sees that in you he may, in his choosing, find someone similar in nature, and without seeing you as a complete women (*meaning seeing you in a relationship where he begins to understand the dynamics on how you interact as a mate*) he may not be able to distinguish between the two, which could cause problems between you and his mate immediately and him eventually once he realizes that he has three mothers instead of just you and his wife's mother; and now with him feeling hemmed in on all sides with no relief in sight may cause him to bail with him possibly repeating the same mistake again until he figures it all out. Remember it's important that sons know the difference, not just for their sake but yours as well because when they don't and they get involve with someone who acts like their mother, possible conflict could occur between you two. Another possible issue coming out of this is the occurrence of spousal abuse (*verbal and/or physical*) steaming from the woman because of her seeing herself in a more authoritative way and from this thinking she may feel that it's ok to slap or hit much in the same way a mother would since now she being the wife replacing you; something I don't think too many of you as mothers would appreciate and another reason why, from our daughter's standpoint, they also need to understand that there is a difference between them being a wife and a mother and what is appropriate behavior for each. I know upon reading this you may feel that this is an universal issue and it is however because again most black women hold the position of being the heads of their homes with no visible male presence (*and sometimes even when they are*), we, so use to being in charge, don't always show our softer side leaving our children with an imbalance point of view. Other circumstances that merit attention when it comes to this issue are again "The Mammie Syndrome" something mentioned earlier, where co-dependency is created between the mother and her children, a situation being mostly responsible for the havoc caused in a lot of our relationships. And because of this strong alliance it's hard for a mate to establish themselves within the union with them constantly competing with their mother-in-laws. (*Additional side note here, giving a clearer explanation as to why these conflicts could occur, being where either because of poor choices in our choosing (abandonment, etc.) or when we do kick the father of our child to curb (from him again either serving his purpose, if the reasons for desiring him were superficial or just to have a child, where we believe the man's presence is not necessary), we, in our attempt to create the ideal man from molding the child to our liking (or the kind of man we would've wanted), feel slighted; as now someone else will be benefiting from the fruits of our labor; a situation that need not to have happened if we had the correct concepts on not only the role in our life our son was suppose to play but the kind of man we should have gotten involved with if we had had good discernment (or a true belief that there are good men out there), with us instead choosing to settle for those who were half ass.*) Now in relation to the wife, usually in these situations the husband looks to her for something that the mother can't provide, which of course is sex, with him leaning on his mother for pretty much everything else. The basis on how to resolve such issues is depended upon who initiated the relationship and what I mean by this is if the man desired the marriage, then he will have to take a stand, with him telling his mother to back off; however if it was the wife who pushed for this, all I can say is that she better start praying with the hopes that Yah intervenes in someway, with her muddling through it until things change. Because the signs were most likely already there that the husband was a "momma's boy" before she got into the marriage she now has to accept the bed she's made for herself. As women a lot of times we enter into things thinking that it is going to be all about us and whatever our men are consumed with, (*children, friends, work, etc.*) is going cease now that we are in the picture. Well for those who think like this, here's a little friendly advice: Don't let your ego play you; just because you're queen bee in your world doesn't mean you'll be in his. Not taking into consideration the strongholds that already exist in his life could leave us with hurt feelings once we realize that things aren't going to change; that's why, in these kinds of situations, when a true visual was given, having realistic expectations are essential if you are to have a successful union. And seeing that you are willing to work with him, may increase his desire to do the same with him now wanting to put more of the focus on **you** (*something else to consider here from doing this is you possibly getting on the mother's good side as well where now because of her seeing that you are not trying to move her out of the way, she encouraging her son to do right by you*). **Now** the flip side of this is when we really do use sex to hook our men knowing we had no intentions of doing anything else, as far as other wifely duties are concerned, then when our husbands turn to their mothers we feel alienated because of us wanting him to let go of what he now thinks he's missing, something I feel again is wrong if you chased after him instead of it being the other way around, which again if that was the case with him chasing you (*with him knowing that's all you do bring*), he'll just have to roll with the punches then until you see things differently. Remember that it cost to be the boss, so if you want to be queen bee then you should be all you need to be with you either bringing it or at least learning how to. And this is what I mean about it not being a good idea to chase after a man, because now you're the one responsible for maintaining it, not him but you. So if he wants a complete woman then that is what you'll have to be. And until you do he will continue to depend on his mother for the other things with her giving you a hard way to go because of you not being able to handle your business like you should when it comes to her baby as well as any future grandchildren you two may have together; something you can't blame her for because of the impression you gave her when you went after her son the way you did, with her thinking that when she turned him over to you, he was being put in good hands (*something that if it was the other way around our mothers could relate too as well*); and with her not seeing that she could cause trouble in your paradise especially if he doesn't back you **up**. (*Something else for women to think about here is us not getting too upset with your man's mother and her blowing you off, if you come to her about him not doing right by you when you got pregnant because in her mind if you were that concerned about what he would or would not do, then you would have made him put a ring on it first before letting it happen! With her also looking at you not so favorably (where now your better judgment is in question) from you not taking into consideration the kind of impact this could eventually have on her now grandchild. And what I mean by this is, is the fact that your child might be left without the presence of a father in their life (or that the animosity between you and her son being so great that the child could end up growing up in a totally dysfunctional environment; something again due to you trying to get her son at any cost) with other concerns coming out of this as well from her wondering how far else you might be willing to go (especially since you were already willing to jeopardize* *another's wellbeing for the sake of love.*)) **So** think twice before using sex as your weapon of choice because you could end up living a miserable existence. Side note to women in these situations; if momma can do it better (*and I'm talking about cooking*) the only choices you may have here are:

a. move out of the way and let her
b. take note, allowing her to show you the tricks of the trade
c. learn to do it better, with the hopes that he will prefer yours over hers then be a bigger person by passing what you know back onto her so she can incorporated some of your ideals into her ways of doing things as well; here, with this option, you now have the opportunity to show what a gracious person you are with all involved seeing that you can bring it as well as them knowing that you initiated it

In this day and time with society putting so much emphasis on sex we as women think that, that is all it takes to keep our men happy, and for some, particularly those who don't know their worth, it is; that's why the line "I'm the one you're sleeping with" works. However for the rest who do know their worth, which are the ones we usually go after, it takes more than that to hold their attention and why when they get bored or disappointed enough with the situation, they will go else where in search of someone who has more substance. So again don't get too comfortable with the idea that what's between your legs is always going save the day; because once it becomes obvious that you lack in everything else it probably won't.

The Black Experience continued, cleaving versus respect, it's not a competition you know

When people couple up, they don't bring just themselves to the relationship, but others who also have special meaning in their lives as well. So making it our business to get along becomes crucial in regards to respecting the other's position. Two things that are mentioned in the bible as it relates to the family, is "a man shall leave his father and mother and be joined to his wife" and "honor thou father and mother that your days maybe long upon the land which the Lord your Yah has given you". So between these two directives, parents and their children's mates are going to have to come to some kind of mutual understanding because it was never meant to be one or the other; spouses are owed a certain amount of consideration because the husband and wife are now partners in crime, just like parents, or in this case the mother, are somewhat responsible for what our mates have become, therefore garnering them **reverence.** (*Side note to wives: In a lot of cases, if it wasn't for her you wouldn't have him, because it was usually from her encouragement that he did the right thing in the first place.*) **So** instead of the mate being threaten by the mother's presence they should be embracing her (*of course that's if you're involved with someone who you feel good about, and if it's otherwise, that's on you again for choosing someone who is lacking, which still doesn't merit disrespect on your part toward the mother*), with you wanting to incorporate her into your **lives.** (*Another side note to all: Remember mates are expendable* (*and can easily be replaced*), *where mothers are not so if your mate wants to continue having a*

healthy bond with her you should not look at it as being a problem.)
As for mothers, taking a step back and allowing these two to
find their way is part of the process in helping your children
further move into adulthood. Seeing the fruits of your labor
through your children should be one of our greatest joys,
because of the validation we receive from knowing that we
did something right. And now with the blending of families
we all should desire a positive outcome, so again, leave the
dysfunction behind and let's make it work. A question to
ponder now for women is one of the things we have always
been told is how a man treats his mother will be an indication
on how he will treat us. So with that being said why is it once
we know that his relationship with her is admirable, as soon
as we enter into coupledome, we want him to kick her to the
curb (*from desiring to be number one*), with the point here being
made if he is willing to do something like this in our behalf
doesn't that put us in the position of him eventually doing the
same to us in the future, whether it be her he returns to or
another woman (*or even worst if you have a son and he, finding
someone of similar qualities such as yourself, requires that he too kicks
you to the curb as well*). Again just something to think about
with you keeping in mind that the love you save may be your
own.

The Black Experience continued, from welfare to the new way of getting paid, my baby's daddy

During the sixties a lot of changes occurred restructuring the
dynamics of our values; one of course was the sexual revolution

with the other being the welfare system. With the former, not having to be accountable became the philosophy of the day while because of the latter an institution of dependency was created making what came out of the former sustainable. Though the purpose of welfare was to help those in need stay afloat, the way it was administered by forcing men out of the home in order for women to receive benefits was not the best route to take; and with a lot of women continuing to have more children in order to receive a better payout, you now have not only a greater number of children being born out of wedlock but a lot men being able to walk away (*because after all why bother if you can't stay*) without having to accept responsibility for their part in it, with a lot of these same men reaping the benefits by getting a cut of the payout as well. Flash forward to the nineties where now both parties are starting to be penalized for such actions, with the government limiting benefits as well as them suddenly wanting our men to take responsibility for their offsprings. However because a lot of our young ladies have grown up under this system (*with them now knowing how to work it*) instead of moving forward, with them going for theirs through education and training, have opted to transfer the foolishness over to other sources with them still having children and getting paid but now though through the men, themselves, with the court systems assisting them in this. So for all you men out there with potential be aware of who you're getting involved with because if you get caught, you will pay (*for all those reading this that was a public service announcement*). Again of course in saying that, a lot of us would think this is a good thing because it should now deter instead of encourage, however with our young men, not having

93

any real guidance (*remember daddy wasn't there*), coupled along with peer pressure to be more than what they are ready to be, they become willing participants in this continued foolishness. Growing up on instilled values that gave us permission to be irresponsible, caused ruthless behavior with a lot our young people feeling that it is ok to do whatever for whatever. So it shouldn't be surprising that our young ladies are going for whoever is getting paid, whether it be ball'ers, entertainers, brothers with a job, and now you are even seeing them pushing up on men with fixed incomes (*see consistency can get you play*). And then once the child support ceases, some mothers turn to their children for the purpose of continuing things. This goes back to the "Mammie Syndrome" with mothers not being able to let go of their children, by either inhibiting them or constantly interfering in their lives. Another issue coming out of this "get yours anyway you can" mentality is women turning to other women. With the number of men who can or are willing to support us decreasing has opened the door for other women, wanting to play the role of a man, to take their place with them also becoming the surrogate parent as well. I know a lot of women who only get involved in lesbian relationships because they know their partner can pay, not because they're really that way. Again the point of all of this is to show how these two entities, welfare and the sexual revolution, failed our society. Even women's lib has had a somewhat adverse effect on things because now you have women, so use to being in charge, who don't know how to properly deal with the dynamics of a relationship leading our men to not wanting to be in one. As for black women, I know this is not entirely our fault that things are the way they are. Going back to all the institutions that kept our people in an oppressed state with a lot of us being forced to take the lead. However, again, once certain paths were opened to us we didn't change the way we played the game. And as far as welfare is concerned, it was us who chose to continue having children for the sake of financial benefit instead becoming more responsible by learning from our mistakes. Because if we had, we might have opted for training and education, something that would've helped us to move forward in a positive way. Then with us making a life for ourselves and our men, knowing that they would have to come correct, with them now having to be responsible before returning or even before getting with us during the initial stages, they might have been motivated to make changes in their own lives. Unfortunately, a lot of what has happened also goes back to the system itself because if the government had been more interested in finding real solutions to poverty (*instead of just putting a band aid on the situation by passing out handouts*) as well as creating solid family units with them offering incentives to the parties **involved** (*like for the man who stays, if he isn't employed or not able to handle his responsibilities adequately, some kind of training to help him get on his feet; and for those who choose not to stay, holding them financially accountable with the woman getting the training or education she needs until she is completely able to stand on her own two feet*) **the** outcome would have been far better than what we have now after the government, waiting until things got out of hand, decided to limit benefits and force fathers to be more responsibility because though the man is now responsible, he still may not be in the home, with the family still torn apart and a lot of us looking to them for financial benefits and them only seeing us as something to pay for.

Last Round, before you let go

When letting go, understanding consequences becomes essential, especially if the possibility of regret for ending the relationship could exist in the future and what I mean by this is, a lot of times when things go awry, we, not really thinking things completely through, make rash decisions; even if it's based on the influence of others, we become vulnerable to a clouded point of view then once we realize that we've made a mistake, we try to return under the thinking that a remorseful spirit is going to be enough without taking into consideration the damage that was done from the hurt we left that other person with. When you leave a relationship clarity should be the utmost part of that decision because once you walk away, with you returning again, you now have given that person the upper hand with them knowing how vulnerable you are; so them being able to set the tone is theirs to set and unless that person understands their part on why things didn't work out the first time around or the love in their heart is so great that it allows them to get past what happened, they may play you like a bad fiddle. Common problems in a relationship that can cause a person to be torn are:

a. Getting into a relationship in the wrong way or for the wrong reasons

b. Not being totally situated in one's life. Here you may be vulnerable to listening to others
c. Having unresolved issues caused by past relationships
d. Lack of knowledge, sometimes when people don't understand the dynamics of a relationship or their feelings, they have a tendency to run away from not knowing how to process things
e. Frustration caused by the lack of communication

(Side note to people who are on the receiving end of this issue, going back to a point made earlier about ignoring the warning signs, sometimes our desire for wanting to be attached can cause us to overlook things that merit attention with us thinking that our love will make it ok; again until things are right they won't be so instead of jumping into a situation with both feet take a step back first to assess things, because you may find that the person you're interested in needs more time and by doing so you could save yourself a lot of heartache later on. Also if you opt to give an ex a second chance, you cannot hold grudges, remember to really start over the slate has to be wiped clean (as well as a sincere desire to fix whatever problems occurred that led to this in the first place) with you letting go of the hurt otherwise it'll be just a matter of time before things fall apart again.) **Now** getting back to the subject at hand something else to consider when leaving a relationship is the possibility of you not finding things in the same state of affairs you left them in if you decide to return. When a person gets hurt they usually turn to other people or things for solace. Even when it's their fault, they still look to others whose shoulder they can cry on, something which, in both cases could bring about them now getting caught up either because of feelings they

have for that other person, though they still care for you, or extra baggage such as a child or physical issues, like STDs, drug or alcohol abuse. If the baggage is a child you will have to be honest with yourself about what you can take on. Knowing that it was you that created the opportunity for someone else to come in when your partner was at their lowest point puts you in the position of having to be the bigger person with you having to work things out with all parties involved; that means being a support system and not someone re-entering back into a relationship under the assumption that it is going to be all about you. Because of the shortage of men, when they become free agents open arms are always there waiting to receive **them** (*something unfortunately why the position of "It's hard to let a fool go" comes into play when attempting to avoid problems like this by keeping the injured party in an emotional tailspin until you are definitely ready to make a clean break. With me saying shame on you and why the suggestion following this text is something you may want to consider before taking this route*). **And** if he's one of the good ones he will want to do the right thing which means you could end up playing third wheel initially; time and the strength of your love being shown, is what it's going to take in order for things to eventually balance themselves out. Trying to compete by bulling your way back into his good graces all while being demanding may cause you greater strife later on and the same goes for emotional issues with him being torn as well. Again if he is a good guy, he is going to want to do the right thing by all parties so forcing him to choose may put you more at a disadvantage, with him now resenting you, than if you had allowed him the freedom to decide for himself on how he wants to do this; because again in his eyes it was your fault that he ran to the arms of someone else anyway and now for the sake of just appeasing you, he has to handle things in a way he'd normally not have had to. Taking responsibility by being gracious, understanding, and patience could earn you brownie points. Now for those whose partners are currently living a destructive lifestyle with them using drugs and alcohol as a source of comfort, if you feel that they're worth the fight, you'll, after regaining their trust, have to get them help with you still having to be patient. But make sure before jumping back into a situation like this that you can really follow through. Pulling the rug up from someone again who took things not in the best way initially isn't right. Everybody deserves to be loved and if the opportunity is there for them to make a clean break in peace then let them. Whatever problems they have now incurred can be worked out once they wake up and realize that they need to pull themselves together. Never go back to an ex based on anything else other than sincerity; guilt and need don't justify a reconciliation. The last issue mentioned in regards to extra baggage is STDs; with us being sexually promiscuous, people have a tendency to use sex as a source of comfort, without the thought of consequence, so then when something like HIV or herpes comes out of it they have now put themselves in the position of being further victimized. So if you're considering getting involved with them again, I suggest you do some serious soul searching with you making sure you understand what you are going to have to deal with; and again by not doing so is not being fair to the other person. Of course a lot of women would turn back around and head in opposite direction when confronted with situations like this. However, and I say this mostly with regards to the first two issues, I have seen, where couples, attempting to reconcile, engulfed in a lot of drama because of the woman, not being able to deal with the extra baggage, constantly tripping (*like the character Melanie from the TV show "The Game" a situation pretty much common in real life, as well as, the foolishness that is Rhianna, Kacrueche Tran and Chris Brown with the love triangle they had going on*); or because she was able to force the man to choose her over the child, baby momma drama, and in cases where an emotional entanglement is the culprit here, the other woman creating problems now that the man and his ex are back together again. Part of the reason for even mentioning this subject at all, especially without putting emphasis on whether you can stand firm on your decision to not come back, is because in most cases our actions are based on where we were at that particular time in our lives, and again because of this, during separation, changes that in all likelihood needed to occur, have taken place in order for things to get where they should be; however again being unprepared for all that has happened while apart is usually where the problem lies. Whether you come back to the perfect scenario or not remember the true essence of a relationship is if the parties involved can stand the rain and one true testament that things are meant to be is that you both will be able to with everything falling into place in spite of it.

Something relating to the previous selection, with a possible solution being suggested here is why not, if you feel that your relationship is at the point where ending things is the next step, consider just giving each other some space first for a while instead of making a complete break (*because sometimes it is not what you do but how you do it*). And by going about things in this manner, you may be able to take this needed time to evaluate the situation more objectively with the other person following suit, something which could now give them an opportunity to get a hand on their emotions with them wanting to trip (*of course something you know would probably cause them to move on abruptly with their actions creating some of the above; and you having to endure it, if you two choose to reconcile*) from seeing this as a loss. Also from this could come a conclusion filled with enlightenment from which you'll either get back together or permanently move on, with you knowing that this was the right thing to do. And if down the line, from you both growing individually, you again decide that you may want to reconcile, you now know what kind of actions to take by not bringing others into your pool of drama. Now in cases, where a person refuses to honor your request, is where the point can be made on why you'd want to do this with you actually being able to show where their being so self-absorb (*with them only being concerned about their own needs and very little about yours*) has become a problem for you. Pain from possible loss can be a difficult proposition to accept, especially when the intended injured party looks at this as something that could've been avoided by maintaining the relationship with both parties working on making things better versus taking a chance on what can come from giving the other space; however, it is important for this person to remember that sometimes people are not always in the same place when they get together (*with one basing their desire to be with a person on true emotion and the other on where they are in their lives at the time the relationship started or like in a lot of cases what they needed from it*); making the possibility of a person deciding if this is where they really should be likely and why the injured person respecting their wishes becomes crucial, if only for the sake of avoiding regret later, once they realize that the reasoning behind this person getting into this wasn't right. Something else to consider here as it relates to the injured party is them understanding that if they have put their best foot forward with them giving it their all, then there is no reason for them to be despondent because true loss always goes with the other person and not those who came correct (*or another way of looking at it, it really maybe them and not you.*)

Reader's Notes

Reader's Notes

Chapter Two

Men

Issues

Introduction, why don't you get it!

Thus far, everything, outside of my introduction to this drama of words, has been dedicated to the ladies. Well fellas it's your turn now and boy ole boy do I have a few bones to pick with you. However though before anything else is said let's get to the heart of the matter; something which involves the lack of understanding of yourself, your purpose and why things shouldn't be this way. All the criticism I have inflicted on my fellow comrades of the female persuasion would've never been necessary if you, yourself, had a clue. We wouldn't be able to run, disrespect, get over on, or blame you, if you acted as a true leader by taking responsibility, understanding your life's purpose, knowing the role you are suppose to be playing in the home, as well as accepting ours, loving us the way you were told to (*meaning the way Christ loved the church*), something which includes you not treating us like some kind of sexual object here for your selfish purposes only. And because of this atrocity of foolishness is why we're in such a mess. Believe it or not you are the ones who are suppose to set the tone, not us but you. And when you don't we as women have to take things into our own hands; women are security oriented creatures (*remember I am one so I know what I'm talking about here*) and need situations that we can count on! Nobody in their right mind is going to follow or submit to a fool, so until you get with the program things are going to stay as they are (*and for that matter may even get worst*) with us continuingly taking over, leaving you behind. Ok now that I have gotten that off my chest let's get this show on the road. Quoting one of my least favorite actresses "Get ready cause it's going to be the bumpy ride".

Though I know you can make it on your own,
    and with all the possibilities surrounding me, I'll always be able to move on.
   It's still part of his plan for us
  To come together,
 Make life together,
Worship him together,
Grow, through struggles we endure, together
 and share a bond so great, that only the creator can break
It's still part of his plan
When asked not to forsake me, even after making mistakes
  Or when respect is no longer and I'm required to understand
 It's still part of his plan
To let love heal
 overlook what can't be changed
  and change what can, because
   though I know you can make it on your own,
    and with all the possibilities surrounding me, I'll always be able to move on,
   It wasn't part of his plan to be,
  two ships passing by,
 individuals with no connection
or enemies whose only purpose is
 to cause each other hurt
  through the makings of . . . .
    jealousy
    dishonesty
     indifference
    abusiveness
     and self-centeredness
    that wasn't the plan
   when I was made
  from me you became
 and together by his covenant, the covenant of marriage, we become one again
so why is it ours?

Understanding Your Purpose

Going back to the beginning of time (*meaning the word*) it was said that you were formed from dust with you being given authority over already existing life, then Yah seeing that all was good decided that a compliment for you was needed so he, after returning you to a state of sleep, took a rib from you, creating woman, your partner, lover and helpmeet (*not your slave but helpmeet*). Being here first you were privy to certain information that allowed you to function as the head (*with it also being since you were here first then why not*) However once you dropped the ball by not stepping up to the plate was the start of all hell breaking loose because of you acting on our suggestion from the partaking of something you knew was forbidden instead of following Yah's directives, something causing us to fall out of His good gracious as well as being cast out of the garden of Eden; Yah, the one who gave you life, authority, and more importantly us, placed the burden of responsibility on your shoulders with you in turn laying blame on us; an action coming from those who consider themselves to be leaders would not do. And just like then with you not being the man you were meant to be you still aren't which is why you continue to suffer with very little sympathy coming your way from us because no matter how many times you have been led to the water you continually reject it by following a foolish heart. Between lust, egotism, and pride you stay in a ball of confusion with you trying to bring us down with you, something again nobody with any kind of sense is going to comply with and why again also you understanding your purpose is so vital to all concern; with the outcome bringing about a guarantee of consistency, peace, and contentment. With purpose you won't chase after every dream or person at whim because what is not for you will not be of interest. Alleviating a lot of hurt that would have otherwise been thrusted on others; which in turn, when happens, could cause bitterness because of disappointment they have now incurred (*I hope you are beginning to see where I am going with this*). Something else mentioned earlier about not knowing oneself is when a person doesn't have a clear understanding of who they are might allow others to define them bringing about the possibility of being led into a multitude of directions and unless the other person or persons of influence involved have sincere motives the confused person could eventually end up living their life for others. All of us are here for a reason and with Yah knowing what that reason is, he is the one we should look to for guidance when the answer is not evident. Because most men have a prideful spirit (*not being able to admit weakness hinders them*) then once things fall apart they turn to those who they see as having direction, which is usually us, without realizing that we too are limited in our own understanding as well. Again women are security oriented creatures so the tendency to send you in a direction that we feel will bring you either security or status (*something which may not necessarily be your purpose*) is likely with you still not feeling a sense of peace from it. Not that we always mean you harm because in most cases we don't, nor is it that we don't sometimes have the answer (*since Yah uses all to the good*) so the possibility is there that we might. But there's a difference between what is used as a vessel and what the actual source is; the source (*meaning Yah*) is where the information comes from not what (*humans or in this case women*) it goes through to get the information to you; and not understanding that is why you find yourself in a constant state of disillusionment. The order of things are Yah, you and us (*explaining why having that relationship with him is so important*). Even if the relationship starts out with us leading you there (*this is where being a vessel comes into play*) things should eventually begin to restructure itself to it's proper configuration and if it doesn't then there is something invalid about the situation. And what I mean by this is if you are operating from that of your own understanding, how you come across to others and the way you live your life will not allow the person you are involved with to trust you enough to relinquish control and submit to you and in the case of the other person, if their motives are not right, they (*with them only wanting someone they feel they can control*) will not allow you to become the man you are suppose to **be**. (*Side note: again going back to the security issue, when a woman starts out holding the cards, giving up power after having it for so long, puts her in a vulnerable place, as well as causing possible resentment because she is now being pushed back into a role that is looked upon by most as being inferior that's why she may only allow you so much leeway, with her withholding certain information as a way of maintaining the upper hand*). **When** things are out of order the door now becomes open for a person to be taken advantage of; part of the risk when you don't take the initiative yourself. Remember no one can argue and win with someone who's already defined, with their direction already set, think about it! Continuing things, under the heading of "Just be a man about it" the following sections delve deeper into all the things that put men behind the eight ball of failure when it comes to life and love.

Who am I, the man in the mirror: Examples you grow up under and why you need to get it together before repeating the same mistakes

Because we as humans didn't jump out the womb completely ready made, a lot of who we are is based on influence and experience. With influence (*meaning upbringing or mentoring*) we pretty much had no choice as to what was feed into our spirit; doing what we were told we showed very little regard for the behind the whys of it all; with us continuing processes that may have never had validity in the first place. Then once we become of age, experience (*something we do have control over*) further shaped our outlook as well as how we respond to future situations. Because influence has some bearing on the kind of experiences we have and our experiences can affect how we again respond in the next ones as well as on the kind of influence we could have on others, whatever was feed initially has to have merit otherwise we can find ourselves in a vicious cycle of negativity. That's why when things go sour and/or the other person's response to our actions isn't exactly what we expected taking a step back for assessment should be our next course of action with us again evaluating the information that was passed down to us. Learning from our mistakes will always be beneficial however learning from other's first before stepping out there could not only save us from heartache but possibly a greater consequence. For example (*something in my opinion I consider to be an overly common recycled scenario*) you, as a young man, grow up in a two parent home knowing that your father is still doing his thing. Seeing your mother (*whether she is suffering silently from his misdeeds or not*) play the "stand by your man" role, (*and from your father's, as well as, other men in your circle, encouragement* (*cause like they say birds of a feather flock together*) *you find someone who has traits similar to that of her* (*or maybe not*) *with you following the same pattern of behavior*) now without taking into account that even though your mother and your wife are similar in nature, the times in which they both grew up in are different with the former maybe then looking more for financial security and the latter looking for not only just that but emotional security as well, which if the case you can expect zero tolerance on the infidelity issue with you losing everything over it once she finds out, again an outcome you'd have never imagined happening from operating under the thinking that this is something you too could do based on what you saw during your own upbringing. Of course upon reading this most men would probably say what's the big deal, I mean you win some you lose some, so just move on and find someone else who works out better in the plan. Well if he really didn't love his wife that might work, but usually in these cases the man does (*it's just he's not aware that he is operating off of a bad concept yet*) so as the story goes, he will definitely be feeling the pain of loss from the consequences of his actions; also even if he does move on, in his mind, no one can really ever replace that now gone person, and because of this he will probably continue doing what got him into hot water initially until "in someway" it is revealed to him that through the course of his life he's been taking a lot of wrong turns with him starting to question all what he believed to be true as well as those who taught it with him choosing not to continue on this path. The "in someway" things that could possibly cause him to change his behavior are:

a. him getting tired of playing (*or in some cases can't anymore*) with him deciding to deal fully with the person he's now currently with.

b. reaping what he's sows with someone doing to him what he has done to others.

c. self reflection or him just wising up after realizing that all that has already happened wasn't that good even during the times he thought it was, meaning once after talking to some of the people (*like his mother or other women*) involved in this foolishness, with him finding out how unhappy they really were, may shake him up or that the man he looked up to was either so much of an butt hole or so full of regret that he decides to change his ways from seeing a future he doesn't want to have.

Another illustration, using some of the elements from the above example goes into what some would consider the definition of a good husband. Here a young man grows up being told (*by no other than his mother mind you*) that what women look for in a man and again how we define what is a good husband, is his ability to provide. Something again that may have worked out perfectly in the past (*then of course maybe not*) but could cause major strife in a marriage now. Because though most women today do appreciate being taken care of they also desire a real relationship as well as having someone who partners with them when it comes to parenting instead of them having to handle this particular aspect alone (*side note: Remember it did take two to create these lives so it should be something you both are jointly involved in*). So if a man's thought processes is coming from that of which he was instructed to do and his now frustrated wife, decides, after numerous threats, to end the marriage with her still getting a piece of his financial pie and him completely being eliminated from the equation because of her replacing him with someone else who fills the void he left empty, he could find himself scratching his head with him asking himself how did all of this happen since from his standpoint he felt that he was doing what a man trying to be a good mate was suppose to do. (*By the way this example is based on a real situation so I'm not just reaching here*). Now the difference between this last illustration and the previous one is what the young man was told wasn't exactly wrong because being a good provider is important, but definitely not all what it takes when it comes to the makings of a good husband (*again just like us being good in bed doesn't make us good wives either, think about it*), while in the case of the infidelity issue, the example this young man grew up under was flat out wrong. Here a change in what the person was lead to believe would have to occur, where as in the other circumstance only a modification in behavior is needed with the person understanding the importance of balance and well roundedness. Now what they both have in common is that what was passed down came from people who lived in a much different time when expectations were more simplistic. Something, if the young man in the second example could have followed if he was married then (*or in this case to his mother*); not taking into consideration the relevance of information being passed down can cost you and the only way it won't is if it is correct; right will always be right no matter what! (*which again if the case, when problems occur in your relationship, you have no other choice but to stand your ground with the other person just having to deal with it)* Bringing me to the main point, that a person should always seek the truth and not take things at face value just because that is all they saw growing up again a lot of what humans do is based on their own understanding and not on the directives that were given to them *(meaning the word)*. Nothing in the bible gives a man permission to cheat, mistreat, beat or mislead, allow himself to be disrespected, not be an example, be unproductive, lead like a tyrant, treat women and children as objects, and not be honorable so why then have you as men taken such liberties like you were? It's because you follow your own thought processes that allows you to think that you can do this, causing others to go into self preservation mode with them making sure that they are not going to be continually put in the position of being taken advantage of. When you look at how a lot of us got together, back in earlier times, it was mostly done through our parents with them deciding very much in the youth of their children's lives, who they were going to marry, which may have been cool if everything was on the up and up as far as everybody playing their part, but what if they were matched up with someone who is lacking or not interested in fulfilling any of their marital duties, with the other person now being stuck in a unhappy union; what do they do? Force issues by controlling the person, leave *(something then that was less of an option because of the arrangement made between the two families)*, continue loving this person in the hopes that it will motivate them to do the right thing? Again what do they do? And this is where you can see how people started making up their own rules just to cope with these ill fated situations and how the start of bad information could've gotten passed down from generation to generation. The one thing that we as his children forget is that our Father is a free will Being, and what he wants from us is based on our own desire to do it. The reason the tree of knowledge was placed in the Garden of Eden was for the purpose of testing us, with Yah wanting to see if we loved him enough to follow his instructions or ourselves and of course we showed him that we love ourselves more which is why again we are in the mess we're in with us still trying to exalt ourselves over the very one who breathe life into us. What we still don't understand is that he gave us information to help get us through things, one of which is the power of love. When a person loves you, you don't have to alter the game to make things work because if the woman values both you and the relationship (*with her being on the same page*) there will already be a readiness in her spirit allowing her to bring it, just like in the same way there should be one in yours too since it was instructed that the initiation of love comes from you first (*with you finding as well as pursuing her*)! Unfortunately some of the reasons for why men choose who they choose, when it comes to their mates, aren't always valid with things like lust, insecurity, ego and image being behind their motivation with them now in turn having to deal with inadequacies inherited from it (*like you choosing a women for her looks only (**from** your needing to be associated with what you know others will desire as well) and her being mean spirited*). Another example that I think kind of brings what I've been talking about home is when you feel that you have to submit to your wife in such a way (*by you giving her the final say*) just to keep the peace in your home. Again if you, as a man, are honorable and have integrity with you demonstrating that you do have her back and value what she brings to the table (*meaning knowledge*) by taking that as well as her concerns into consideration, she should be able to trust your judgment enough for that not to be necessary. Staying silent for the sake of keeping the peace can again cost you with the lost of your manhood (*something that can cause you to step out on her in times when you need to be re-affirmed*) and more than that if she is wrong; because when things fall apart who in the home is going to pick up the pieces if you are not use to doing it, the kids! Whether you like it or not order will eventually have to be re-established for things to get back on track. Remember there's a reason you were delegated the position of headship, so don't allow the fear of drama to keep you in the zone of ineffectiveness an action that could bring about an outcome of regret later. For a of lot men dealing with their spirituality is something that they try to avoid, because of feelings of suspicion resulting from what they have seen as being hypocritical; with the constant failure of leadership in the church itself as well as a sometimes alienation created by the sense of onesidedness being at the center of it. However such as that is though, having familiarity with what you feel is questionable, is important because after all how can you say something is wrong if you really don't know what it's about. Again being born with a limited understanding (*or having trouble believing anything beyond what we see*) is what causes us, as humans to thirst for greater reference, so then the question here is why not start with what's already been given; for what's in the word (*countless examples*) is something we can all benefit from with it showing us what Yah is really about as it relates to us, his children; then once clarity begins to come into play with things unfolding, a relationship with him is now possible with him revealing to us our purpose as well as a providence of real **guidance** (*something our parents sometimes failed in giving us while growing up because of their own human frailties; again going back to why, when we become of age, we need time to really sort things out, with us cleansing ourselves of the bad and retaining the good before fully jumping into life*). **And** having a valid compass to depend on can help tremendously in this process as we continue on our journey into self-discovery. Now outside of doing this another suggestion to consider is finding examples who are living their lives in accordance to the way it is said to with you then doing a stare and compare; something that could bring about the opportunity for you to not only see how others handle similar situations but to break away from the constant reinforcement of what you are use to as well as possibly eliminating some of the justification on what you think is ok to do.

Lust vs Insecurity, Just Be a Man About it: Why Honesty is the Best Policy

Self gravitation and image (*or how one views themselves as well as how we want others to view us*) are usually the driving forces behind lust and insecurity with them both in turn feeding off each other. Lust (*something being based on one's own desires without regard to the other person's needs and feelings*) is considered a selfish, non lasting emotion with it fleeting once the trill is gone or for whatever reason (*sexual or physical attributes*) a person was desired has been met and/or no longer exist, as well as to elevate a person's status based on who they associate with (*or again to continue the process of inflating a person's ego with them choosing people who they feel match up to their level*). And because of this is where the problem lies. When you look at a person lustfully you cheat yourself as well as the other person out a of deeper connection and since you only saw things from the standpoint of having your immediate needs met initially you never found out if this could be something worth sticking around for. Something that could definitely come back to haunt you once you've ran through several meaningless relationships and realize that you have nothing to fall back on from burning bridges with these people (*something again that happens when you cowardly bail out of the relationship to avoid drama from starting something you didn't want to finish*) Other things that could come out of this:

a. Parenting issues, if a child is now involved, with you being attached to someone you no longer desire, with you incurring baby momma drama if you decide to move on or you being miserable if you stay with you blaming the situation (or the child as you now become indifferent) instead of yourself.

b. A consequence of possible drama coming about if the person can't let go with them causing major grief in your next relationship.

c. You having unrealistic expectations, under the thinking that everybody should be perfect without you considering that you yourself could fall short eventually.

(here you may go from person to person with you never having the ability to settle down.)

d. A bad reputation because of you being viewed as a love them and leave them type, something again that could definitely bite you in the butt when you finally find someone you really care about or if you decide to take the high road with you having to prove to people, you previously discarded, that you have changed your ways if you desire to reach back to your past. *(example: One of the candidates from the Ultimate Merger, Charles Parker, the Player)*

With the possibility of a person now being damage goods from your foolishness occurring, *(things like low self esteem, hurt, etc)* you taking responsibility for your actions by admitting the errors of your ways, with you letting the person know that they deserve better than someone who didn't have the correct motives when you went after them, can save you from a lot of the above. And again by doing this, the person may be able to get past the disappointment of things not working out as well as her seeing that, even though you were wrong, you do have some sort of conscience, something that could work out favorable for you especially if you both decide to be just friends *(and again what you should have started out being in the first place)*. Remember women are not just here for your pleasure, but to compliment you so what they bring to the table should be not only valued but long lasting as well. With lust being a selfish emotion, it is very easy to make what you admire in a person *(physical attributes or actions)* the essence of the relationship; even to the point of being at the expense of another's well being. Take for example you being drawn to a person because of them having large breast, now for you that's great but for them it's a burden with the discomfort it causes from her having back problems. So when she expresses a desire to alleviate some of the problem by getting a reduction you protest with you forcing her to choose between having you around with continued interest in the relationship or losing you because of her doing something that will physically benefit her in the long run; and this is where how lustful desires hurting others comes in. When you decide to pursue a person, with things getting past the dating stage, there should be more than what initially drew you to them keeping you there (*things such as a deeper emotional connection, friendship, and a general understanding of commitment (remember for better or worst, right) all of which are ingredients that make a relationship what it should be*). Knowing different factors (*some of which are out of our control, like illness, accidents, resources, etc*) can change the dynamics of what you are use to, it should be a given that you would be expected to weather the storm and not be looking to run in another direction when they do. And for this reason, when you can't, is why we lose interest in you sexually because of your lack of regard for whatever effects us. Of course I can hear a lot of men say well the same thing goes for women too with us wanting you to be on all time, which again I say, we are wrong as well for continuing to expect something that may not be all that feasible **anymore**. (*In reference to both parties, a side note: Purposely doing things or using your assets just to keep a person around is stupid for everything that's already been mentioned concerning this subject thus far, because what you did to get them is what you have to continue doing to keep them so think long and hard* *before putting yourself out like that; I mean doing what you do (like using your attributes) just to reel them in then stopping (or letting yourself go afterwards) once you feel you got them is tricking with bad karma being a mug if the person continues desiring it.* When dating we tend to put our best foot forward without realizing that what the other person might be basing their decision to commit on is the picture we've painted (with all the wining and dining as well as sexual enticing) so to minimize future problems, it's probably best to let the person know that what you are doing now is only possible because you don't have to deal with the responsibilities of a true relationship that way the person can decide if they want to continue with the relationship or just move on.) **Ok** getting back to lustful desires, if you are one of those who likes to jump into relationships on the basis of lust, while still in the dating stage, ask yourself the question if whatever you like about this person now changes would there still be enough of the other qualities there to hold your attention; if the answer is no, then maybe this is not someone you should be pursuing anything further with. And as far as for men, in committed relationships, who find themselves in the predicament of being involved with someone for the wrong reasons, being honest with yourself first is part of the process of taking responsibility for your decision with you then in turn trying to make it work by finding other things (*like the development of a true friendship*) that could help create the kind of union that will allow you to stay committed. Now as for insecurity, something mentioned earlier, it derives from how you view yourself with it causing you to choose people who you think will elevate you in someway (*something also mentioned as it relates to lust*). And because of this you may find yourself putting the cart before the horse with you going after the person you desire without being ready for them. Outcomes resulting from this are:

a. You putting a reign on the person for the purpose of playing catch up or to bring them down to your level with the possibility of mental and physical abuse now being involved. (*this happens when the other person is still growing with you being afraid of losing them.*)

b. You trying to keep up until you can't with her now looking at you as being a lame, something that could cause you both lost and ridicule or you now being lead by the person once they know that you don't have a clue with you again looking for someone else to validate you once things get old

Getting yourself to a healthy mindset can serve you well because once you feel comfortable in your own skin you won't look for people to make you feel good about yourself but instead for those who appreciate you as the person you are. Also when you have your ducks in a row you now have the advantage of being able to pick and choose because the world is more open to you with you not limiting yourself to certain people based on what they bring to the table. Another thing here is you won't waste other's time. In a lot instances when we look to a person to elevate us once we've come into our own we no longer show interest causing the other person heartache. But if you wait until you feel more secure about yourself and where you are, you won't need to go there and the only reason you would is if it is based on genuine admiration. If you find yourself constantly drawn to people for this reason think about not approaching them as possible romantic partners first but instead as friends with you letting them know that even though you are attracted to them you are still working on yourself (*the advantage of expressing interest at the beginning is that you let her know where your head is at and that because you see her as someone who deserves the best you want to make sure you can be all the man she needs you to be with you really bringing it, something again she'll definitely appreciate*) and by doing this you give yourself buying time to get your house in order (*whether it be self-esteem issues or direction*) with them seeing the person you have grown into, something that could possibly bring about a greater admiration on their part. And if it turns out that your desires for this person are fleeting at best (*again lust*) or based on where you were at the time then you haven't lost anything with you being able to walk away peacefully without drama from not being romantically attached to them. Of course waiting until you get yourself together first before stepping to us is really the best option because you don't have to deal with the possible complications of being distracted. Speaking of friendships because how we see ourselves is so intertwined with who we choose to associate with, taking a step back and observing the direction of others becomes important with us making sure that the same road they are traveling on is the same one we want to follow and not allow the hold that might exist already (*when it comes to these kinds of relationships*) to redirect us from the path that we should be taking. Insecure people usually look to those close to them (*friends, families, and lovers*) for guidance with friends being the main source of influence; something in most cases can be a little dangerous because just like you as a person are still finding yourself so are usually they with them seeing things from a limited point of view as well. And this is how you becoming your own person can benefit you greatly with the opportunity of being lead astray minimized. However since the issue at hand is about those who are still works in progress here are a few words of advice I'd like to pass on. First, outside of observing, ask yourself what is the reason behind your desiring support in this way:

a. Is it because of a desire to be liked or accepted.
b. You feeling that those you're looking to follow have more knowledge than you with you hoping for the same results because of the success that was brought about for them.
c. Fear of failure, with you being able to blame someone else if things go wrong.
d. You being bullied into going along with the flow.
e. Fear of growing with you staying with what is familiar instead of stepping out of your comfort zone.

Secondly, what are the true motives behind the people who are advising you, I mean is it really more in the form of what's in your best interest or theirs. And thirdly, does their council (*as it relates to you*) have the same merit (*or does the outcome they achieved work for what you need to happen*). If the answers are b, yes and yes then you should be good to go with you knowing that it is coming from someone who is qualified to advise you because; they have the knowledge as well as a proven track record that it works; understands that this is about you, so, outside of them being happy for you, self gain wouldn't apply; and more importantly their advice relates to your particular situation something which if it didn't the other two wouldn't matter. Now as far as the other choices are concerned being forced to learn from your mistakes through the many failures and disappointments you've again incurred from all the bad advice you've received from people who either were too consumed with themselves with them, in their own way, looking for validation by putting you in the position of following them even though they knew they were wrong, or just like bringing another person down because they can since it's obvious that you are easy prey. Men needing approval from other men, especially those who didn't have a strong male influence growing up, is increasing becoming an issue; with you looking for something from your peers what they can't provide which is a true male role model and because of this is why your life is in constant turmoil. When you are able to distinguish the difference between what you most likely really need (*a father figure*) and what was designed to be a support system or camaraderie you will stop depending so heavily on the wrong ones and seek out situations that can provide both. The father (*or any male figure who you felt let you down*) that should have been there had his own issues (*you know like something maybe relating to the subject being discussed now— insecurity and lust*) just like you have yours and unless you've learned what not to do with you being a better man than him by handling YOURS, you really have no other choice but to make peace with the fact that he was just doing what he knew to do (*from what he saw*), encouraged to do (*by those around him who he thought knew*), or felt was best to do (*from his own understanding or lack of faith that things could've work themselves out if he attempted to see it through*). And again in saying this the same applies to your mother, because of her not considering the consequences of creating life (*a child she was stuck caring for alone with the possibly of her being bitter because of it*) with someone who was either lacking or that she herself may have been lusting after and why seeking guidance from the one (*Yah your spiritual Father, someone who will always be there when all else fails*) who wanted you here is what you should be doing, again we are vessels with Him using us (*his children*), to accomplish his goal through creation. The problem however though is we usually look to people (*something we can see*) for love and acceptance not understanding that when things don't happen the way we expected them to with it being either non existent or negatively being part of it, we wonder around like lost puppies, going from person to person, trying to find what we need (*through romantic attachments or friendships*) with us still being left with the feeling that something is missing and this is where Yah comes in revealing to us (*once we decide to seek him out*) all we need to know and why developing that relationship becomes important, with it being something that leads us out of uncertainty. Being the only one you can be sure of, who you know wants nothing but the best for his children, Yah expects us to love and support each other in the same way he does so it stands to reason that having a balanced outlook is what we should be aiming for when dealing with the world around us with consideration for all being the basis in which how we go about achieving it. That's why there is no such thing as "one without the other" when it comes to brotherly and romantic love; we all serve a purpose and when the people (*whether it be a love interests, family or friends*) you interact with try to tell you otherwise, their motives are usually suspect with them wanting to control you for the purpose of self gain. This happens a lot in situations where a person is caught in the middle of the old (*people who want you to stay where you are*) and new (*those who want you to move on*). And depending on the outcome of what they want you to do is what determines validity. For instance when you (*having the ability to pull ladies with your running buddies reaping the benefits as well*) decide to settle down (*with them knowing you are serious and that the person you're trying to do this with is the right one*) they (*meaning your friends*) will either accept your decision with you now in turn being able to incorporate them into your world as a committed man or try to discourage you because of them still wanting to reap the benefits from riding your jock. Ok now let's takes this same scenario, and flip it around with the young lady being ok with you still continuing your friendships (*something now that would be incorporated into the relationship*). If she cares about your feelings and sees that a happy median can be established between the two (*in this kind of example because your friends have already accepted you wanting to settle down then it shouldn't be a problem with this all working out*) she should be open to it however if she is selfish, with her being more concern about herself than you, she will want you to drop them regardless of their support with you now possibly being under her thumb through the duration of your relationship. In both situations under the first outcomes your happiness was considered and because of this you have the ability to bridge these alliances into a unified front. Other benefit coming out of this are:

a. With you now leading by example, you might be able to influence your buddies in such a way that their outlook about commitment might change if ever the opportunity is presented to them, something that could happen if your girl has a few friends she wants to set them up with (*or maybe not*).

b. With your girl seeing that this can be a positive outcome, she could share her experiences with her friends under the hopes that maybe they could cut the men in their lives some slack, as it relates to their buddies.

c. And in reference to a point made earlier from statement (a) about her friends interacting with yours, just being able to bridge both sets of friends together creating a completely balanced environment.

d. If you or your buddies never give your girl a reason for concern, greater trust between the parties can be achieve.

Now in regards to the second outcomes, both parties demonstrated that it is all about them getting theirs. So whoever decides to come out the box like that is probably the one that needs to be cut loose and if it's both, then maybe it's time to start from scratch with you getting new friends and a new girl. Using another example, showing how a friend's discouragement can actually be of benefit to you without total loss being involved. In this particular situation, using commitment issues again as the backdrop, the person advising you knows you well enough to see that you may not be ready for what you are trying to do right now (*like with you still wanting to be a player and the young lady wanting to commit*) or that the person may not be good for you at all with the friend being able to provide information to support this from what they have already seen as far as the other person's actions goes. And by doing this, with them encouraging you not to move so quickly (*at this time*) they are not saying that this is something you should never consider doing but in fact are trying to save you from possible future drama if you go forward with it; something I feel is a little different than a person discouraging you altogether because of their own selfish motives. Now under circumstances where certain alliances or situations no longer work for you, changes in who you associate with may need to occur in order for you to grow especially when moving away from the negative becomes imperative. Again this is where when another person recognizing this comes in with them encouraging you to find your path. Always remember for the reason there's a season with people and/or situations being placed in our lives for a specific purpose then once that purpose has been served we can continue through our journey passing on what was given to us (*inspiration, knowledge, friendship, love etc.*) to others we encounter along the way or even to those who were left behind with the door being open if they choose to positively move forward, knowing that all who have touched our lives helped shaped us in some form or fashion, that's why "one without the other" never fits into the scheme of life because no one person can be all things to anybody and the one who can instructed us to be there for each **other**. (*Side note: If you choose not to look back by not being a blessing whatever you've gained from those who blessed you will become your curse from burning bridges and since you would have nothing to* *fall back on when tragedy strikes, with no one being there to help you out of your now mess, you will be stuck in it so again don't allow your own stupidity or other's foolish influences trick you into thinking that you don't have to be appreciative).* **Allowing** another's voice or voices to dictate your actions is one of the problems with insecure people with them being unable to think for themselves. And as far as women are concern, if you can't stand on your own as a man, with you needing a support system to back you up on every decision, any relationship you involve yourself in will sink. Again no woman in her right mind wants a man who can't think for himself and if she does, she wants to be the one running the show not those outside of her influence (*also keep in mind if she does you best believe a deal has already been cut, with them all being in cahoots with each other*). Understanding why you need not be a follower can help keep you from falling prey to it, even in those times when you have been designated as one (*remember we all can't be chiefs*) you should always be seen as someone who possesses true confidence, being comfortable in your skin with you still having the ability to take a stand when you have to; and what this represents is the epitome of someone who gets us, because when we see a man who knows who he is it draws us to him; just like in the same way it does you, with you greatly admiring the way we carry ourselves. Something again unfortunately that can turn into a problem for us both when inequality is placed between us, because again due to your lacking. Another pet peeves I have with men is the fact on how you trip because of our so called high standards. As women we have a right to expect you to have your act **together** (*I mean with it being you that came after us. Now to* *women who are reading this as well, if you chased after him again, what you got is what you get, understanding that maybe this is why he didn't approach you initially because he knew where he wasn't so don't complain now because of you being disappointed*), **with** it being crazy on your part to think that we should accept you on the basis of you just existing; this is especially true as it relates to BLACK MEN, with you focusing too much on what other races have to or don't have to do, something that blindsides you when trying to complete with them, then once after you realize that they still have their foot on your throat (*a state that will probably always exist because of the world we live in*) you use the excuse that you can't do any better. Again understanding why you need to make the best of whatever tools that are available to you will get you far because when people see that you are at least putting forth some kind of effort, they (*the vessel*) will want to help **you**. (*Side note: One of the advantages of getting into the word is because not only is it a book that never loses relevance, (and I say that because one of the excuses that we, as a people, have on why we lag behind everybody else when it comes to education is because of the disparity in resources when compared to theirs, something which would not be an issue when it comes to the bible) but after you get through properly interpreting name after name, city after city, etc. you should be a scholar, and again from reading it with you gaining a better understanding of what is expected of you as a human being might motivate you in such a way that you will now be more humble and less prideful (with you getting out of yourself), something that needs to happen in order for you to see the vision*). **Operating** under the thought processes that we, as women, should continue bailing you out is what keeps you under our thumb; creating a state of frustration that can again in turn cause you to continually make bad decisions just to prove your how much of a man you really are. Another issue relating to this is the lack of community in our own **race** (*you know with us not being able to work together to make something happen ourselves instead of looking to those on the outside to reach back and help us, I mean why is it that black men can come together for doing things like selling drugs but not for pursuing positive ventures, because it's not like you don't have the ability to do better you just choose not to*) **and** this is where a good support system comes in, something that this particular discussion is about; with again the point being made about why you need to have the right people around you, people who not only are looking out for your best interest with them understanding that you should be your own person but understand everything that is done should be for the good of all and if that is not possible, with you not finding people who want to support these kinds of endeavors, then do it yourself with you seeking the purpose from **within.** (*Side note: Something else to consider when you are put in the position of having to move away from those who no longer fit into your scheme of life, is even though they are no longer part of your life sending a pray back their way, that Yah will work on them in the same way he is working on you might allow the relationship to come back together again in the future. Letting go of those you love or think highly of can be difficult with it causing you to feel guilty because of where you are now with you either going back to what drove you out or never looking back from you not knowing how to handle the situation, however when you turn it over to the one who can really get their attention, you will be able to accept whatever happens without regret. Again whether you are a blessing by being an example or you just letting Yah handle it, you've made a difference which is really the* *purpose anyway.*) **Now** again getting back to the subject at hand, in regards to inequality, with women doing it for ourselves and you not is creating a greater wedge between us, sometimes to the point of where you try to make us pay for it. Remember it's from your own foolish thinking (*or again those around you who have influence over you*) that causes you to see the glass as being half empty instead of half full. Nothing worth having will every be easy to obtain, it takes ingenuity, hustle, desire along with a few other things to make what you want happen to happen. But it won't if all you do is nothing but spend time feeling sorry for yourself with you wanting us to join your little pity party. Things like not going to school, standing on the corner, being unproductive, laying around on somebody else's couch while eating their food, or using drugs, alcohol, or other means of distraction like women accomplishes what? (You answer that) Then when you see us take the initiative ourselves you feel betrayed. And even in situations where you do appreciate our efforts, you, now becoming uncomfortable with us moving ahead as well as being afraid of losing us, use things like abuse (*physical or mental*), manipulation (*drama of some kind*), or discouragement to control us. I know of men who only get involve with wwas (*or women with assets*) just for the purpose of keeping them under their reign (*or the almighty chase, with their ego getting the ultimate boost from knowing that they can have and concur someone like this*); which to me is stupid, I mean you got with the person because you appreciated the fact that she has something on her mind (*or other attributes such as looks, charm, etc. you considered to be a draw*) so why then is it a problem now (*even in cases where she makes you number one with her either pulling* *back with her encouraging you to move forward or her forsaking all for you this still happens*) and this, in my personal opinion, is where I feel if you can't handle the game then you should've left it along, wasting others time when they could have been captivated by someone who really understands the plan with them also being able to back up what they say, by bringing it. And I'm not just talking about status **either** (*cause there are a lot insecure men out there that have that but still don't have a clue with them wanting it to be about them all the time or them only using it as the basis of defining who they are without understanding that there is more to a man than his accomplishments, a subject coming up*) **but** you being ok with where you are in your life, something if the case, will either motivate you to seek future romantic partners who have the same like minds or, because of your own positive self-worth, you allowing others to be who they are with you supporting them to the fullest and that's what anybody with a good head on their shoulder wants. Now flipping the situation around, even men, when they get involve with a woman who is constantly trying to hold them back because of their own issues can be a pain and it is only because of them not being a man about it that would allow her to be able to do this, something mentioned earlier about men who have attributes that draw us but are still insecure (*or misinformed about what a real man is, something again that usually happens when there is an absence of a proper male figure during their formative years*) with them allowing themselves to become prey to someone else's foolishness. Example, because of you not being popular during your youth (*with you being studious*) you missed out socially with you later (*from a professional standpoint*) coming into your own so now you meet someone, who is seemingly hot with her being someone you always aspired to be with, however, because she is looking for someone to bail her out of her troubles (*or continue putting up with her drama*) is why she gravitates toward you, a person she knows she can persuade into seeing things her way and this is where the problems begin as she is now able to wrangle you around her finger, causing you to be distracted with you now possibly putting everything you worked so hard for in jeopardy, as well as, alienating all those who have always had your back. In situations like this, with you being aware of your own **shortcomings** (*you know like lack of experience (something that could have been avoided if you again understood the importance of friendship with you gaining discernment by learning people before moving forward with anything serious) or your attempting to recapture a lost youth by filling the void you created from what didn't happen then while you were pursuing your goals*) **you** can create an environment of heighten insecurity for yourself causing those you draw to see you as a sucker and from this happening you allow these same people, who may have nothing at all (*or sometimes just as much which if the case, you two are still equal so what is she bringing that you don't already have*) going for themselves to dictate the direction of your life. Again because women are security oriented creatures uncertainty is something that can drives us to take the kind of actions that will ensure that we don't end up coming up short later; explaining why when potential is not evident, we'll choose to bypass; a stance that might seem hard, but something we (*who have any sense*) sometimes have to take because of the repercussions when we don't, like us being stuck holding the bag if you fall short (*whether it be emotional or financial issues, or* *the children you walked away from*). Now for those who think the answer is taking the easy way out by dealing with people who are in the same boat as you because of you trying to avoid the enviable (*like responsibility or the betterment of yourself*) think again because unless you are 100% sure that neither of you will ever change your position on moving forward, you could find yourself on opposite ends of the spectrum once one of you decides that you want more from your life than what you are now experiencing, that's why settling doesn't work either because the basis of it is only temporary with it bringing about disillusionment. Other issues relating to insecurity are:

a. You allowing yourself to be put in the middle of your mate and immediate family's (*namely your mother*) drama; remember you need them both so be a man and take a stand with you setting the proper boundaries. And by doing this they will have no other choice but to work out their differences because if they don't then they will lose you.

b. Something relating to (a) is you not being able to do right by your child. Here you need to properly set the tone between your new woman and your baby's momma. And if it is just the baby's momma you are dealing with put yourself in the position that allows you stand up to her when you need to by handling your business in the first place that way you will have the leverage you need to check her if you have to. Also, in regards to your kids, learn to sensitively put your foot down with them seeing that there is still room in your life for them (*meaning anybody you involve yourself with knows that your kids are important to you*) and from doing so you will create the proper example by showing balance. The end result from all of this is you not carrying the burden of regret later from you punking out.

c. Understanding that there's a difference between being nice and being a wimp; with wimps following those who over rule them and nice people following their conscience, doing what's right with them letting the chips fall where they may. Something again important to understand because a lot of times men think that just keeping the peace is the solution to conflicts when in reality all they are doing is avoiding the inevitable (*future problems*) when things get out of hand instead of putting a stop to it from the onset.

d. Not being able to be honest with your mate. Remember what's done in the dark will always come to light; but if you bring it to light first yourself, you have a chance to get past it from being a man about it. And what I mean by this is if you have done something or are doing something that needs to be addressed instead of hiding behind the fear of consequence, or attempting to drop the ball by not taking responsibility for your actions at all, come clean, with you doing it not only on the hope that the person or persons involved will just get past it (*with them seeing that you have learned from your mistakes and want to come correct*) but for desiring to know that there is true validity in your relationship because when you get involved with someone and that person expects the utmost from you, they should be also expected to take the good with the bad and if they can't then they themselves are loving you on condition only, something that will never last anyway (*with you now walking on thin ice, a condition that could eventually cause the foundation of your relationship to cave in under the pressure of what was never resolved*). Also know that it is not love (*but lack of respect you have for that person*) when you attempt to make a fool out of someone, just to protect yourself, by making them believe one thing when it is really something else, especially when everybody else knows the real deal.

e. If you don't have a ring on it, them why are you letting her run the show by allowing her to bully you into something (*like a relationship*) when you are not ready yet for this kind of commitment with them throwing up whatever they've done for you in your face. In situations like this unless you pushed first with your forcing them to do something they weren't comfortable with (*like sex*), they can't make you feel obligated to anything they want because they had a choice and could have walked away by not doing it. A lot of times we as women, when trying to hook a man, throw ourselves at you with us doing things we think are going get you to commit to us then when you don't move fast enough for us we start trying to make you feel guilty about it as if it were you who forced us to do these things. Though it takes two to tangle and you shouldn't have accepted or done anything that you didn't want to be obligated too, still doesn't give the other person the right to hold you solely accountable (*of course you know regardless of whether or not you and her continue the relationship if a child is now part of the picture you will still have to do right by it; with you (again if you choose not to continue things) hopefully teaching the young lady a lesson that using a child to get a man does not always work with her also discouraging others not to do the same stupid thing; see the possible blessing in this).* **When** a person does this you know where they stand (*with them trying to be manipulative*) so stop accepting whatever is being offered with you also putting them on notice that you are fully aware of what they are doing, an action that should help in preventing you from being made into the bad guy because of things not going exactly the way she planned. And by doing this you will see once and for all if they are perpetrating or just don't know better, which if it is the latter they will leave it alone respecting your position, however if it is the former, it is probably best to move on (*unless they do it first*) because if you don't they will continue with you eventually getting caught up; something now that will be on you.

f. Something else also relating to the above as well as to the example concerning the young man allowing someone else to map him out. Again because we as women have been taught to believe that we have all the answers, a lot of times we come into relationships under the thinking that it is ok to remake you; something that might've worked if she picked you up from out of the gutter with her enhancing you (*again something that could still end up being temporary because once you come into your own you probably will be gone*) but what if you were already handling your business or she doesn't even have a hand on her own situation, what then? And this is where you knowing your worth comes in with you putting your foot **down** (*remember the old saying if you don't stand for something you will fall for anything, a situation that puts us as women in an unstable environment as well that's why we have to keep a reign on you, to protect our own interest since we already know how easy it is* (*with you being so gullible*) *for someone else with a better game to come along and sweep you away*) **Again** there is nothing wrong with opening yourself to the ideas of others but when you allow someone to come in and completely rearrange your life, especially without merit, disillusionment will eventually occur because of her trying to define someone who is already defined. And if none of what she is trying to do works for you it will spell disaster. Whether you are allowing this to happen because of again fear of loss, you not feeling good about yourself or naïve thinking, in the long run all could suffer from it with you feeling more alienated than what you originally started out being, and her digging a hole for herself once she realizes that she can't carry the ball anymore because of her constantly running the show. In relationships, being considerate of each other feelings is important that's why as women we should care how you feel with us respecting all that you bring to the table as well; also as women we should desire something more than a blank canvas, because it says very little about us to want you to be working from nothing outside of just your visual presence. So again know your worth and once you do they will too and if they still don't get it then keep the faith and move on to someone who will recognize it.

Another illustration using point (b) as a reference shows how both lust and insecurity intertwine. Here a man, seeing someone he desires, pursues and who's heart he eventually captures; all of which is fine except, he has unfinished business with his kids from a previous relationship, where for the most part, he's not been part of their lives, something he was on his way to correcting until he jumped into another relationship with him knowing the spot he is putting the other person in because of the environment of animosity that already exist between him and his kids. Now based on his security level he'll do:

a. Nothing, with him just moving forward with the relationship, hoping that things will either work themselves out or him just chucking the whole idea of reconciling with his kids altogether because of his priorities changing as well as him being afraid of now possibly losing the relationship.
b. Make her aware of the situation with him letting the chips fall where they may because of him wanting to do the right thing by his children.

Whether this behavior is intentional or just you doing what comes naturally, basing things on either of these two factors will cause nothing but **grief** (*like resentment from us especially when you jump into a permanent relationship from it with you not* *taking any kind responsibility for your actions, something if you did like by fessing up initially (and before emotions start taking hold where now we have a choice on whether we want to be bothered or not) could have at least saved you from our raft)* **to** all in the long run because of you being more concerned about getting the girl than handling your business. So again think before acting on something that may only be temporary before it leaves you empty and full of regret.

Chapter Three

Men Issues Continued

The Dating Game

Tell Me Why Do You Play the Way You Play

Introduction

Utilizing repetition by revisiting certain topics over and over again, hopefully in someway shows validity with the dots being connected as we go. Each of what is considered relevant should be treated like individual pieces of the puzzle when once constructed gives us a complete picture as to what this thing called life is really about. And again here is where things like friendship and romance come into play with them working together to create the ideal union. However because of your (*meaning men*) limited point of view (*with you only seeing women as sex objects*) is why you don't always look at things this way, something I hope will change after these last two sections.

Yes Again, why can't we be friends?

As already mentioned, because men look at friendship between the sexes as something of no real benefit to them they usually choose not to pursue it. From the wining and dining, or being good ole what's his name (*when we need a shoulder to cry on or man size favor*) there seems to be more of a feeling of being taken for granted than true appreciation, especially if the lady of their affections walks off into the sunset with someone else. A sentiment any perpetrator could relate to from the knowing that they have just been duped (*or beaten by their own game*). And I say this because for the most part outside of being that shoulder or person they can depend on when needed (*you know for things like the lifting of heavy furniture*) you are not being a friend but a possible romantic interest and that's the problem. Friends are people you kick it with, mutually be there for, sometimes share with if you choose to (*not because you have to*) who support you in your endeavors as well as give it to you straight because they know what you need to hear (*without fear of loss because they are not depending on you like that*) and who encourage you to go for yours with the only reward being in it for them is seeing you happy; not people you are trying to sleep and/or have a romantic future with (*unless you both, during your period of platonic-ness, come to the same conclusion that this is something you want*); confusing the two is why you end up being on the short end of the stick because again of you not getting past seeing us in any other way than sexual. Some of the advantages for changing your perspective are:

a. Getting to know someone without faking the funk, here you can be yourself and not have to put on airs by pretending or over killing to make a good impression.

b. Setting boundaries, by not doing boyfriend work without boyfriend pay, of course here you are able to minimize someone else's ability to take advantage of **you** (*you know with all that wining and dining stuff, unless that is how you roll regardless of your status with this person, something which if the case I'm sure she wouldn't be too mad about*), **as** well as being able to check them when they get into the "it's all about me" mindset, with you reminding them that this is a platonic relationship therefore you are a free agent not restricted by their presence. (*Side note: When you do something like this, the other person sees that you've got balls. And because of this you* *will garner respect as well as a possible second look, with you making it clear that you are not a chump. Remember when people think they can play you, regard for you will be reduced with them turning to someone else who they feel can hold their own.*)

c. Valuable insight when it comes to the opposite sex, due to you now associating with those who have the inside track to a woman's thought processes. Also by gaining a better understanding of what women are about, may help in you not being so quick to judge or downgrade us because of you seeing things from our perspective.

d. Again going back to point (a) you getting an opportunity to look before you leap, if you were interested in the person initially from a romantic standpoint; with you now gaining better insight while better acquainting yourself with this person; something giving you a surer footing on whether there's still good enough reason to consider pursuing this endeavor or not. This also applies to her as well so if you two should decide to go there you both have valid information to base your decision on.

e. Relating to (a and b) not being restricted to whom you choose to associated with. Since you are not courting this person, you don't have to explain who you direct your interest toward, giving you the opportunity to do a stare and compare. Also by showing your female friend how you interact with other women, gives her a glimpse of what she might get or how you have evolved from when you two first met (*I mean with all that insight you've gained, something should've resulted from it*) if you both do decide to go down that romantic road in the future.

f. Clarity as to what you do want in a woman as well as growth in your outlook, like maybe appreciating someone not just because they are pretty (*something that men do when choosing who they associate with*) And what I mean by this is a lot of times because you do look at us as potential romantic partners when you approach us you base your decision on what turns you on sexually, leaving those who don't behind. However when your motives are more about friendship than sexual conquest, your social circle is open to a wider range of different types of women with you eventually being able to give them romantic consideration as well.

g. Discipline (*something that should already exist since you have no business doing anything before marriage anyway*) because you learn the art of self control as well as an acquired appreciation for some of our other qualities outside of the physical; something that can be of great benefit in times when you can't be with that person from a sexual standpoint, such as when long distance or physical barriers come into play because you have a broader focus. Something else to consider as well is when you do get into a serious relationship just knowing how to handle yourself in the company of other women without feeling insecure about it from learning to see women as just people instead of sexual objects. (*Side Note to this, as this particular point relates to age difference and romantic interest. Though not encouraged, there are times when men of a certain age find themselves attractive to young ladies (not women) of a certain age, with of course the problem being it totally inappropriate on his part. However fast forward ten years later when something like this could be considered ok for both parties if these feelings still exist, you see how someone, employing great discernment, could dodge a serious bullet by not giving into his initial urges, as well as respect from the wisdom he displayed; with it all saying how choosing platonicness in situations such as this could work more in your favor. Something a few celebrities should have learned (R Kelly with him ALLEGEDLY having a relationship with a then 15 year old Aaliyah) with people like Jay-Z, who currently is married to Beyonce, twelve years his junior, getting (along with the likes of Damon Dash as well who too was involved with a 22 year old Aaliyah at the time of her death.)*

h. Being able to show other potential romantic partners the kind of person you are with them seeing that you don't chase after everything with a skirt on (*something that gives the statement about sexual objects in point (g) relevance*); here if you are in a situation where you are hanging out with a female friend and you see someone you are interested in you can introduce yourself openly with her knowing that not every women in your life is a girlfriend.

i. Relating to (d) if the other person comes to you desiring to take it there with you not being interested, you have an opportunity to explain with true answers. And from that, if they accept your rejection, you can possible give her some insight about what may not be working for her, something that could help her out later as far as someone else goes.

j. Possible future hookups with her (*or them if there is more than one*) introducing you to some of their friends as well as you returning the favor by doing the same.

k. And one of the most important benefits of friendship, is the foundation it provides. If your relationship becomes permanent you have something else to fall back on when things like physical attributes, passion or financial factors are not exactly where they were when things originally started out; giving you both the ability to continue things without thought. Also if you choose to move forward from things being casual, the likelihood of being involved in a long courtship is minimized because you already know a lot about each other (*a definite benefit with you being able to jump straight into marriage and yes sex*), something not as easy to happen when you start out from a romantic standpoint initially from having to go through the getting to know them process first before even considering marriage; again something which if it doesn't work out could leave one or both of you with a lot of hurt feelings and regrets. Now on the other side of this is if things don't move to marriage, from this alliance, you will always have a great friendship.

Of course we pretty much know that the obvious outcomes would be the opposite of from whatever's listed above if friendships was not part of the picture when pursuing romance, with the ultimate solution being you waiting on Yah to direct **you** (*something that even out trumps friendship unless it is incorporated into the answer with him pointing to someone already* *in your cycle, which in most cases he does, hence explaining why I keep putting such a great emphasis on it.*) **The** only problem here is you not following through by allowing selfish desires to get in the way of what you should be doing, like committing to the person instead of stringing them along until you decide to do the right thing. (*Something again that can happen even when you base your choice on whom you know causally*). In dating there is always a risk involved because of the other's unknown motives, with them either being honorable (*mutual understanding and acceptance of whatever happens, a true relationship, or upfront friendship with you knowing where you stand, so if you go there by attempting to win her affections anyway when you've already been told it was a no go makes it all on you*) or again self serving (*using others to get theirs, designating someone as the standby person when the main one isn't available, keeping someone under their thumb even when they know they don't want the other person with them requiring the utmost loyalty from them*), something either which can change based on how things flow (*you know like with you starting out looking for sex then suddenly things taking a turn with you now being interested in really getting to know her*). And since some kind of interaction has to occur in order for you to get from point a to point b, etc., places you in a state of vulnerability because of whatever it took to get you there. That's why offsetting things becomes important by putting in the kind of work (*things like being charming, generous, or us giving it up, something that relates to women because after all that's what you are usually trying to get us to do, etc.*) that allows you to achieve your set goals sooner (*you know like moving on to the next conquest*); something that, if the other person catches on or them being the type who knows how to use their Yah given assets in a way that gains her sole benefit, gives them the ammunition they need to justify playing you by again stringing you along for as long as they can with you having nothing to show for it (*because zero times anything always equals zero*) except being put in the dreaded friend z**one** (*something that wouldn't have happen if you weren't either trying to get over yourself or slowed your roll by not over extending yourself without making sure that this is something you should be doing or can do first; something again that happens in the same way for women, when things do go in your favor, with us thinking that sexual or even financial favors will win your affection with you again in turn reducing us down to just a booty call or nothing at all*). **Because** one garners disillusionment while the other incurs bad karma (*cause like they say what goes around comes around*), in the long run, nobody really wins here from this kind of situation; giving merit as to why men should come correct with you either keeping things causal initially until you have valid reasons to move forward or just waiting for a higher directive from the One who knows not only who will receive you but who's right for you as well. (*Additional side note here: In reference to dating and courtship as it relates to the bible, there is none with this actually being a man made custom (just like arranged marriages were before that), something I feel explains why inconsistent outcomes result from it, giving credence to all that's mentioned throughout this section.*)

Waiting on Yah

Starting from where the previous section left off, we get into why when moving ahead with things, (*or the subject at hand dating*) without a word from Yah can spell disaster. From all the advantages of just being platonic, it is easy to see the kind of safety net a person can provide for themselves when trying to avoid the possible pitfalls of romance with it allowing you to slow things down while still being able to enjoy the company of the opposite sex until all factors that need to happen fall into place. Whether it be you or the other person needing to:

a. Grow up a little more.
b. Work out issues that you have grown up under that need to be addressed such as abuse (*physical or emotional*), abandonment, general self-esteem, etc.
c. Find your true destiny or satisfactory completion of goals, such as educational or career.
d. Further your personal development (*not the same as growing up where ideals and concepts need to change or achieving goals*). Here you may have your direction but need to see what the world has to offer first by getting out of your comfort zone for a while.
e. Get past previous failed relationships with you clearly understanding what happened and the part you played in it, as well as, working out whatever you inherited from them (*like baby momma or daddy drama, financial, etc.*) so you can move forward in a positive way.

All these things, as mentioned before, can be considered baggage (*or issues*) when coming into a relationship (*or just casual dating with the other person now being burdened with them as well*). Something that might've been avoided all together if we had chosen the right path. And what I mean by this is even though whatever Yah has for us will happen, we still have a choice in how it comes about with whatever motivations (*selfishness, ego, insecurity, lust, loneliness, genuine emotion, etc.*) being behind our decisions playing an important part in what we do like jumping into situations before Yah has worked things out. Take for example, a person still heartbroken from the ending of a previous relationship with them jumping back into the game anyway (*something due to loneliness*) before completely letting go of the past. Now the new person not understanding why things aren't moving along like they **should** (*a situation occurring because the heartbroken person hasn't fully dealt with the ending of the other relationship, consequently making them emotionally unavailable as well as being stuck in the past*); **so** as time continues with the situation becoming more and more frustrating, the new person, having enough, decides to move on. And from this, with this person no longer being in the picture, the heartbroken person is forced to do some serious soul searching with them finally tackling the issues at hand as it relates to their own internal conflicts, the previous relationship, etc., something that could lead them to either attempt to reconcile with the old person or come to terms that what did happen was actually best with them now being able to open themselves up to love **again** (*a situation that could bring them back to the door steps of the new person if they find that they really do care about the person with them trying to make amends by explaining what the problem was in hopes that the new person will graciously* (**meaning without holding a grudge or totally becoming untrusting of them**) *take them back, something that could happen if the heartbroken person is willing to go the extra mile to prove that they're genuine; something again that would not have* *had to occur if they had waited until they were actually over their ex before pursuing other romantic ventures.)* **Now** the question here is would Yah have encouraged this person to do something like this knowing that the person wasn't healed yet or hadn't gained the proper understanding of their own behavior? And that's the point! Taking this example even further *(from the many different ways on how this scenario could've been worked)*, what if the heartbroken person had temporarily reconciled with the old person and a pregnancy came out of it with them finding out after they got back with the new person *(again see the problem here)*. If they had waited until Yah had freed them up emotionally before getting back out there like that it could have been a smoother **transition** *(something again that also applies if they had met the new person during this process with them using platonic friendship as a safety net until they knew that they were ready for something else, here the new person could be a vessel being used to help this person through their storm with emotional support)* **Now** if the ending of this example had been written in such a way showing the broken hearted person and the new person getting together, consider what could've happened under the wrong circumstances, possible drama *(from the extra baggage incurred or just having to go through additional changes before things are finally settled)*. All saying again why a word from Yah is so important because he already knows what it is going to take to get things to it's best possible outcome. In any given situation timing is everything, whether it be for opening doors, the changing of one's behavior or outlook, cleaning house, etc.; transformation of some kind maybe necessary for again things to fall into place. And because we are not always aware of this *(or too selfish to care)* we, as humans, never take into consideration the mess we could possibly create for ourselves as well as for others until it happens with us now having to do what we should have done originally which is to resolve whatever needed to be resolved. By understanding the consequences of the decisions we make helps validate the importance of having integrity something which I feel is the starting point of knowing that Yah is giving you a word. For whatever Yah wants to happen he will create an open path for it to come about. (*Side note: With us all lacking in someway, forces us to learn from our mistakes as we travel down life's journey. So it is understandable why those who read this would object to the simple concept of just getting a word from Yah because until you are at a point when you realize this you would've had to have lived a whole lot of life; something which again is part of the process because without having these experiences you would have nothing to base your decisions on what not to do on. All saying that experience really is the best teacher. However, once you've gotten to the place where you no longer want to work off of your own understanding from the end results constantly being that of unsatisfactory is where consideration of other sources, such as again a word from Yah should come in allowing you to operate differently with you also having the ability to provide guidance to others because of the wisdom now you gained.*)

The Importance of being one with oneself

As we delve further into the subject of dating, the issue of solitude or alone-ness comes into play with the question being why do men have such a difficult time seeing value in solitude. I know a lot of what defines a man (*or in general how society defines him outside of his financial status*) is on his ability to capture the attention of women (*with the more the merrier being all what one aspires to achieve*). And because of this the chase becomes that much more important even if it's without thought or regard for anything else (*like whether what you are pursuing is of benefit to you or not since the basis of your decisions derive from a desire for validation or approval of some kind from others.*) A circumstance unavoidable because of how life is set up with us born into a state of dependency, relying on those around us for physical and emotional support. And as we grow this process continues with us again relying on friendships as well as other casual encounters for additional support systems, all of which pushes us away from ourselves with us in turn (*when we do come of age*) basing everything we do on what we have already been working off of. That's why getting out of this kind of comfort zone becomes essential in furthering our development; with us not only exploring life through various experiences but just for taking time to discover ourselves. And by being afraid to do so we hinder the chance of coming from under the influence of others as well as reliance on their presence in such a way that without them we feel inadequate or insecure about ourselves. Other benefits from learning to be one with oneself are:

a. Of course the obvious one is hearing Yah's voice, with you being able to receive his word. Something of which, as you will see, greatly relates to the advantages that follow.

b. Self-confidence with you not being afraid of lost if certain emotional or physical relationships don't pan out because you understand that no one is the end all to anything with them filling a void only really Yah can fill; giving you all that you need to move forward.

c. Getting a clear understanding of what your direction is because again of you hearing your own voice.

d. Learning the importance of both discernment or self-reflection with you understanding that what works for you, something you need when people around you are constantly trying to get into your ear with them keeping you in a state of confusion; something, that when does happens, will have you always doubting yourself with you not being able to make decisions on your own or them being completely made for you.

e. Discipline by learning to keep yourself; something that becomes important when you need to avoid certain situations (like when you are no longer interested in a person) because of you not starting something you couldn't finish. Here you won't be using people for short term purposes until you emotionally get back on your feet; something that could possibly block you (*with the ugliness of it all being incorporated into it*) from long term possibilities when you do meet someone you really are interested in.

f. Lastly just learning to enjoy getting to know you, with you finding out that it is ok not to always need to be around people all the time.

Now flipping this around the aftermath of getting with someone just because of loneliness. Oh yeah cause this is a subject in itself with a continued summary below:

a. Settling, with you being a ten and her being a two. Again being lonely you may not pay much attention to whether or not you and the person you're pursuing are truly compatible from being so desperate to have companionship with you finding yourself in a very unsatisfying union once the honeymoon stage is over. And the danger in this is if other people are involved, like children, other family members, etc. with them probably being the ones who suffer from this ill fated situation the most because of them having to endure someone who may not be all that interested in making things work, outside of maintaining whatever they have with you if they can (*cause remember you're the one seen as having the upper hand, with you having the assets or heighten attributes*). Also, if you do decide to go forward with this kind of relationship, you will have no other choice but to compromise with you probably having to accommodate to them (*or coming down to their level*) instead of it being the other way around, since there is a greater likelihood that you jumped in with both feet because of how you came into the situation with your state of affairs being out of order, so again don't let loneliness blindside you with you making a mistake you might regret later.

b. Silence is golden, saying too much too soon. Now here this point relates to not only situations where a person is lonely but also if the person is just ready to settle down with them not putting a lot of thought into whom their getting involved with. In both cases things become a problem when you tell people that your main objective is to get married (*for whatever reason*) and this person, if they are in a desperate state of affairs themselves, now being able to set their sights on getting you, even to the point of faking the funk by playing whatever role they think you want them to play, with them changing the game once things become official and you again being stuck in a situation that may not be as satisfying as you were led to believing it would be. Then when someone comes along that you really could've had something positive with you will either have to fight to free yourself from this ill fated union or accept the bed you made for yourself by putting on a good face with you trying to make it work. Again until you have a clear view of the situation it might be best not to be so open about your wanting to plant roots, with you seeing how things go first, and as time goes on and things fall into place you then can start being more open about wanting to settle down. Something else to consider here is when you come to a woman with this kind of offer up front she is expecting you to follow through so even if you decide that things are not a go with you and her, she will probably have no problem throwing up in your face that you expressed different intentions at the beginning of things than what you are talking about now with her again being able to make you feel guilty about it, something that can get you roped into the relationship further or just you having to endure drama from it. So again think twice about opening your mouth before making sure you can really follow **through**. (*Again remember women were made to be in* *a relationship, because that's what Yah created us for, where as with you, you need motivation with the conditions having to be right for you to commit PROPERLY and the only way to get around this is you having a good sense of duty with you being able to take responsibility for your actions by making the best of things; which requires a lot of compromise on your part and her being the type of person who appreciates your efforts. Something which could've been avoided if you didn't come into things under the wrong thought processes.)* **Since** loneliness is a temporary state, there are a number of ways of combating it, like just in general with you participating in **life** (*whether it be family and friends* (*only if applicable though because in most cases these two group are part of the problem with them constantly bugging you to move on to someone else. Now in reference to what one should consider as being positive associates, are those of wise council who would advise that you be in a good emotional place first before taking on any new ventures*), *charitable work, school, or church*); **anything** that allows you to keep your mind off what isn't happening for you right now (*like again with you not having someone to call your own*) something that could eventually bring you to a point where you now see things more clearly.

c. Incorporating the philosophy of "if you can't love the one you want then love the one you're with" into your life when distance comes into play. This again is part of the discipline issue with you as a person not allowing loneliness to cause you to make the wrong move through infidelity (*whether it be emotional or physical*) just because the person you desire to be with is not in close vicinity.

Because not only is it disrespectful to your relationship but to the other person as well with you again using them on the basis of something that's only temporary. Here, it is important to remember that in all we do there is consequences, so don't think you can slip in and out of things without it having some kind of effect later.

Ego Issues

Whether a person is lacking or not, there are times when men get involved with women solely for the purpose of being able to exalt themselves over them; any way at any cost. Not taking away from your desiring to be head, however, when you find yourself choosing to pursue only those you can control or keep under your thumb, you are not looking to be loved but to be worshiped or idolized and that is something not yours to happen. Again just like women, don't have all the answers either nor can be everything to any one person, the same goes for you that's why you fall short when you don't understand this. And when you look to people who bring nothing to the table outside of just admiration, you now have additional weight on your shoulders, with you carrying the whole load (*because after all you wanted to be head honcho with you now knowing what it means when people say that it cost to be the boss*) Remember we are here to be your helpmeet not just your cheerleader; so don't be intimidated by those who compliment you or again fear of lost because what is yours will either appreciate you or come back if they feel a need to find their own way. Being egotistical is nothing different than from being insecure with you needing validation of some kind in order to function, something as far as the other person is concerned becomes a great burden with them either having to hold back their own attributes or becoming over accommodating just to appease you. And if they get to the point (*if they haven't abandon ship already*) where they feel that they have had enough is when the games begin with them playing you like a bad fiddle, because they have learned how to work you, with them stroking you just such all while getting theirs. End results from this are:

a. Possible physical or emotional abuse when you see that you can't get a hand on the situation any other way. Something else relating to this is when you try to take on the role of that of your mate's parent (*or in this case the father*) with you finding yourself competing with him, desiring the same kind of reverence he receives. Something considered a common problem amongst egotistical or dominating partners who feel they have a right to move in on paternal (*or maternal*) territory; with them trying to replace all others of influence. It's important to remember that there is a difference between being a partner and parent with you understanding your role and them theirs; certain authority will never be yours just like certain privileges will never be theirs, with you both needing to respect the other's position in order to achieve a positive alliance. Something that should start with you since you're the one pursuing their child. And by doing so possible consideration for your feelings will be granted (*once they know that you really do have their baby's best interest at heart*) with it in turn benefiting you in the future when you find yourself in similar circumstances with you standing in their shoes.

b. Again carrying the burden if the other person involved is lacking with them bringing very little to the table. Here you may find yourself needing some kind of relief through affairs because of self inflicted pressure you now have put yourself under.

c. Because of your need for constant stroking, having multiple women in your life all at once with it now becoming an obsession. Because this is a selfish endeavor you will never be satisfied with you attempting to maintain a primary relationship all while stepping out on this person. And since it really isn't about the other person **anyway** (*with them not loving you correctly and they themselves being the prize, is why these affairs are meaningless with you only interested in stringing those who don't get this along*) **they** could find themselves cheated with you being as well because you never learned to keep your ego in check as well as appreciating what you already have at home. Another issue coming out of not only this but point (d) as well is if your mate, desiring to keep your ego in check, refuses to pacify this kind of behavior by either ignoring or belittling you; with the likelihood of you seeking others out who are willing to play by your rules being great (*yes so obligating*); and again from this you still will only be looking at it as temporary solace with you never truly desiring to leave your mate, all from working off the hope that one day it will eventually be them who you'll be receiving this kind of admiration from. Now if it's just about the chase or challenge of it all (*which in most cases it is*), you will become relentless about winning your intended target over; with you in turn (*if you are able to pull this off with you getting her attention*) humiliating her by pulling the rug out from under her.

d. Finding yourself alienated from women because of this constant need to be number one with us not wanting to be bothered because of all the stress we garner from it. Remember relationships are about relating, something that requires a lot of give and take interaction; so if you desire to truly be loved realize you got to give in order to get and not just what you think we want either; like just your presence, or financial security (*cause again remember money can't always buy you love*). A lot of times men think that their financial achievements will be the deal breaker when it comes to winning our affections, without realizing that for the most part we desire those who are little more well rounded, someone we can enjoy life with whether it be the simple things or not, feel emotionally secure with (*through your devotion, attentiveness, etc.*) as well as someone we know will handle his business (*now of course a touch of humility thrown in doesn't hurt here either*). And by treating us like some kind of object that you feel can be bought does nothing more than create a wedge between you and us with us never appreciating any of your efforts.

Further showing the damaging efforts of being egoistical, we use the plight of a young lady caught in the middle of two reigning forces, her family and her mate. Where she, use to the finer things in life, because of her well to do background, has married a man who isn't because he didn't and because of this, when things like birthdays or holidays come around, with her family's displays of extravagances continuing, tensions arise; something of which brings about both resentment as well as great dismay to the young lady's husband with him feeling inadequate because of his own lackings. Again being fully aware of what he can't do for her he expresses great desire, during these times, that the family discontinue these kind of gestures with the young lady now feeling a sense of obligation to her husband by not accepting their tokens of love. Of course upon reading this I'm sure a lot of men can relate to this scenario, with them feeling that her family should back off by letting him be the man. Which I would agree, if they were throwing it up in his face that he can't provide for their daughter the way they could; were always interfering in their relationship by jumping in when things are not how they feel they should be (*you know like maybe offering to help out with the down payment for a house because they don't want their baby living in a shack or what they perceive as being one*); or if they were competing with **him** (*something I think is a little different than throwing things in a person's face where here they are doing it because of their own insecurities with it being more about them than him, something that the first condition isn't about with them attacking the husband due to possible dislike in their daughter's choosing of him*); **none** of which was mentioned in this particular example. Going back to something mentioned earlier as it relates to the cleaving issue, when people get married a definite transition should be transpiring with both parties looking to each other for the meeting of needs, but again as also mentioned in the, "Women and the games we play" section, it was never intended to be one or the other with either party totally disconnecting themselves from their respective support **systems** (*such as family and friends, with the former usually being the ones we'd turn to for helping us pick up the pieces again, if things go a bust (like divorce or loss from death). That's why when someone asks you to choose like this you have to question their motives with you wondering what would happen if things got out of hand with you now being left holding the bag from all that has gone wrong, whether it be financial, emotional, etc. Always beware, for when you give into an egoistical person like this (by going along with their foolishness) you put yourself in the position of always having to be over accommodating with their thirst becoming never ending, and constantly needing to be quenched.*)) **Now** getting back to the subject at hand, as far as, the young lady's parents (*or anybody parents for that matter*) are concerned it will always be their prerogative to spoil their children, no matter what age, with it being solely up to the person (*or the child*) directly involved if it continues or not. Again as long as what they are doing is nothing more than just an act of love, and not a personal attack on you, or an opportunity for your mate to use this as a way of discounting you (*something which if she is then you need to check her by reminding her that you are who you are with you only being able to do what you can do, so either take it or leave it. Cause she didn't have to accept your offer by accepting your hand if she didn't like your plans. An additional side note here with a suggestion to the benefactor: One way of avoiding these kinds of dramas is with you requesting that your loved ones give money or gift certificates instead of an actual gift, that way if your mate wants to do something special for you the opportunity will* *now be there for him to do so without worrying about budding heads with your family and if he doesn't or can't due to being under limited circumstances you can take what your folks gave you buying what you want with it without feeling guilty about it.)* **you** should not be offended since this is not about you in the first place. Which is the problem with people who have big egos, because of them demanding to be number one all the time, they treat anyone who they feel can possible outshine them in someway as a threat with them wanting the person or persons eliminated from the picture *(or limiting them in someway)*; something also mentioned earlier about women who seem to have a difficult time dealing with a man's mother with it all being about her ego as well. Now what both reigning parties are suppose to have in common is their love for the one seemingly real victim here, *(or in this particular situation, the wife)*, with them both wanting nothing but the best for her and as long as she appreciates her husband's efforts he should be ok with whatever her family does for their daughter; with him hoping that when the time comes he can do the same for his own **family** *(or maybe not if this isn't the goal because of his beliefs, something which still doesn't give him the right to control his wife in this way)*. **A** lot of families have been torn apart just on basis of whatever issues a person's mates **has** *(something which makes no sense, since there should be a bringing together of families with them both benefiting from each other's presence)*; something that when things like tragedy *(death or catastrophic illness)* **occur** may leave the other person with feelings of regret or a continued riff possibly being passed down to the couple's offsprings with them now having to choose between their parents *(if they desire to have a relationship with their estranged family)* and those they were never allowed to have any involvement with, with them now having to go behind the backs of their parents just to establish some kind of relationship, (*and in the case where they don't choose to pursue things, the additional support systems they could miss out on.*) and all because of the so called injured party (*or in this case the husband*) not being able to handle that he got with someone who came from a more affluent background than himself. Whether the person marries you on the basis of where you are now or where you will be in the future, you should already know that they love you regardless with her not expecting from you what you can't **do**. (*Side note: This example gives credence to the point about what happens when you don't know what you're stepping to and why it's important to assess things first, something leading us into the "What You Get is What You Got" section.*) **Something** else to consider here, that may not necessarily relate to this example but in some ways more to point (c) with the possibility of this kind of outcome still occurring in either case and that is the stroking of one's ego through false flattery. In situations like this when a person is frustrated (*whether justified or not*) they can now become open to another's advances with them possibly allowing themselves to get caught up. Something that could spell even more disaster for them, than the one they betrayed (*if they find themselves getting something they never bargained for*) with it possibly turning into a nightmare or them being unable to reconcile the situation they left behind as well as any financial issues they now might incur if the other person was depended upon them in that way. For example what if a man is away on a business trip and he meets a young lady. Conversing with her, she lets him know that she is interested (*though she's already aware of him* *being attached*), saying something to effect that if he was her man, she would never let him out of her sight; something which for him at the time sounds very flattering because of her holding him in such high regard that she would not want anyone else to have access to him. Now without really thinking about what she is actually saying here he goes for it with things heating up and him getting caught up leaving his marriage; so with them being together now, she keeps her promise by not letting him out of her sight; with him now again having to endure a possible crazy or overly possessive person. And the real kicker here is the person he left for her, trusted him enough to give him the kind of space that allowed him to associate with others, something which he took for granted; a consequence causing him to now be under constant watch patrol with him not being able to breathe in peace without her clearance; an action that could affect not only how he interacts with other people in social environments but also his **job** (*because of stress brought on from having to deal with an insecure person* (*something all resulting from her meeting him on a business trip with her now being fully aware of what he is capable of doing; and I guess that's why they say payback can be a mutha huh!*)). **And** this is what happens when a person allows themselves to be open to something first without thought to what they are being open to, as well as why they were being open to it in the first place with them probably thinking that something must have been lacking on the home front when this all started because of someone other than their mate making them feel more desired. Not to say that their mate didn't but again maybe because of the person possibly being unrealistic about **things** (*like maybe them not being able to cater to him on a regular basis like he would've* *wanted them too. Something again that relates to what I was saying earlier about expectations and that in order to get you have to give with you as the receiver making sure that the giver is in the position to do so with them not being over burden by what you demand of them; all of which requiring that you operate under the thought processes that they are only one person.*) **they** interpret their nonchalant attitude for unconcern, not realizing again that it can't always be about them. So now the person has to deal with a lot of drama that they wouldn't have had to deal with if they had been realistic themselves.

What you Got is What you Get

With us coming off of issues relating to a man's ego and what all involved could incur from it, I now want to talk about those who attempt to play savior or go for those they feel they can change (*or bring up to speed by reinventing them to fit their specifications*) with them seeking projects (*or women who are considered works in progress*); something that could leave them disappointed as well as betrayed once that person decides to move on. But first before going any further with this, let's get into the specifics of what this particular section is about for a minute with you understanding that when you pursue a person (*with you already being aware of their issues*) you can't expect changes to occur just on the basis of you now being committed to them. Because unless the person sees value in your point of view they will fight you tooth and nail with them becoming **resentful** (*from you not being able to accept them for who they are with you again already knowing what they* *were about in the first place; something whether you realize it or not might have been the main reason for them committing to you, under the impression that you did; something that even if you have already expressed dislike for whatever doesn't work for you, you still proceeded with things, with this again coming across to them as being total acceptance in their eyes; all saying that you should've walked away initially with you instead getting caught up)* **and** you frustrated from realizing that what you are offering isn't enough to win this person over to your side with them being obliging. Remember since it was you who pursued them, then it is you who bears the burden of having to adapt *(with the same being for women, when we chase after you)* and what I mean by this is when you look at the dynamics of courting, with you as a man seeing something *(or someone, you know like the way we really should see each other, even though we don't)* you like, with you approaching them; now from this you make it your business to win this person over all hoping that in time that they will not only grow to appreciate your efforts with them developing caring feelings for you but also become open to things you desire *(like you not wanting us to be so consumed with our careers with us giving you more of our time)* versus things just being about her with her only being interested in getting her needs met. And this is how courting or the dating process **works** *(something most see as being quite a bit of a gamble with it being a fifty-fifty chance that things will go in their favor; which is one of the problems with dating from the possibility of someone giving more than they receive occurring, with one or both parties getting hurt in the process)*, **and** why I said that the person doing the pursuing bears the burden of adjustment. So if the object of your desires sole motivation for being with you is based on what your doing benefiting them in someway you will have a rough time of **it** (*unless things change with them starting to care about you, something in all likelihood may never happen because of how things started out with her already having an agenda. Side note: With dating it usually entails the luck of the draw (or a word from Yah with him directing you to the right one) with you having to go through several women first before meeting someone you not only actually feel comfortable enough being yourself with (something being the same for them too) but also, as it relates to any efforts you make during the course of your getting acquainted with them, being ok about it; so when you do it behooves you not to take them or the situation for granted*) **with** them having very little regard for anything **else** (*which again is why compatibility becomes important here with you making sure that you and this person are on the same page; something that should start with friendship with things developing at the kind of pace that allows you to see if there's an existence of it between you two*); **however** if you find yourself in a fortunate enough situation where the person is compatible with you or cares enough about you with her showing the kind of consideration that makes all this workable, well then I guess you know that you have hit the jackpot with you feeling a sigh of relief that she too is willing to carry the burden of being adaptable as well. But again you should be looking to accept the person for who they are with them doing the same. Though compromise is essential for a relationship to survive no one should have to alter the essence of who they are just to make this happen with you both assessing things properly before proceeding any further from your desiring to take things to the next level. Other issues coming out of pursuing people like this are:

a. Is again the 10 to 2 complex with you choosing people you know are not on your level, with you now being able to get by with as little as possible because of a feeling of **arrogance**. (*And in cases, where we, as women pursue you* (*or accept your offer when we know that your are lacking in some way*) *for this same reason, with it usually being for the purpose of trying to control you under the thinking that we're your best option*). **Here** the opportunity of being able to take advantage of things comes into play, where, if the person you've pursued does make demands about desiring something more, you attempt to belittle them by reminding them that you are the one holding the cards and that they should be grateful for your attention; something which if you are successful in convincing them of this will now allow you to set whatever plans you have for them into action. And one of the major problems with this, outside of all the possibilities of a person being able to manipulate another, is you cheating yourself out of a truly satisfying relationship with you not pursuing someone already on your level; from you just either being plain lazy with you not wanting to live up to your own potential thereby avoiding another's critical commentary (*or from your own fear of failure*) or wanting to reinvent someone else with your motives being that, once the pursued person is where you want them to be they will become so appreciative of your efforts that they will now be indebted to you (*something again which as already mentioned*) could backfire on you if the remade person decides that they now want to explore other options or turns into a monster with you now having to endure someone who brings new meaning to the phrase "be careful what you ask for cause you just might get it". A lot of times in our quest to enhance (*or detract*) a person's attributes we forget what initially drew us to them (*something which when does happen the essence of them is now lost*) and since they allowed you to do this they also don't think much about it either with them easily discarding these qualities therefore becoming something you not only don't know but may not even want anymore.

b. The pursued person feeling overburden by the demands of trying to be something they're not. And out of this two things can happen with one being the person now becoming resentful toward you for not accepting them for themselves or them being left with their self esteem further reduced because of feelings of failure from not living up to your expectations.

c. Disappointment on your part when you, believing that you have all the answers with you feeling that you can save someone from their misery and things not turning out that way when changes you desire don't come about as quickly as you would've like. This happens a lot in cases where you get involve with people who are temporarily at their lowest point (*like from heart break or some other emotional related disappointment*), with you now seeing this as your chance to slip in and make things better. Remember there's a process that we must all go through to get past the storms that occur in our lives before we are fully able to move on to something positive (*that's why they say in Yah's time and not ours, with him knowing what needs to transpire first*) so rushing a person because of your own desires serves no one well with the possibility of you being left with egg on your face happening in a big ole way from things not working out in your favor. And if you are successful in achieving the outcome you desire it may have came about but at a price with you having to put up with a lot drama before seeing any of it happen.

d. You attempting to remake a person, even before you yourself are where you should be, with you being completely settled. In situations like this, everything is based on where you are right now with you, as a person, still evolving. And the problem with this (*something also mentioned in point a*) is you realizing that it may have been best to have left well enough alone once you come to terms with the fact that there was nothing wrong with the person in the first place, with the actually problem being you (*again something relating to your own insecurities*). Example, you trying to impress people not worth the time of day with you putting pressure on someone else to follow suit then once you finally get it, the damage has already been done with the person going through unnecessary changes as well as possible emotional abuse from your insistence that they do this.

Seeing those we pursue (*or who's offer we chose to accept*) as just objects is why we believe we can pull off changing them (*or manipulate into doing what we want, something which still entails the person having to change in order for them to be able to successfully do this without regret or conscience*), with us replacing Yah's version of the story on how their life should unfold with ours. However, going back to something mentioned earlier about getting through one's storm before moving on to something better, without understanding the dynamics of another's journey as well as their purpose, we help in delaying a person's growth from trying to take things into our own hands by simply imposing our desires on them; something causing them to eventually have to fallback, with them now going through what they should have gone through initially in order to get things on track again, leading them to where they should be. Whether the outcome involves self acceptance with certain experiences providing the kind of insight that allows them to be comfortable with all of who they are or just for the sake of gaining the proper perspective on how they should see life; something again we (*the would be offender of this crime*) could benefit from as well, with us witnessing the transformation for ourselves (*with it bringing us needed insight also*) or being a vessel that Yah uses to accomplish his will and not **ours** (*again something which is going to fit into his plan anyway once whatever we're trying to get this person to do blows up in their face from consequences they have now incurred, all relating to what I just mentioned about a person having to fallback*); **something** all of which is the point since the real focus here should be for the bettering (*or cleaning house*) of ourselves, as individuals, instead of worrying about someone else with us redirecting them by deciding what we think they should do or be; with the true motivations behind our actions stemming from our own lackings with us attempting to remedy it through others.

THEY SAY BIRDS OF A FEATHER FLOCK TOGETER
WITH IT BEING SINCE YOU ASSOCIATE WITH THOSE
WHO YOU FEEL ARE LACKING THEN WHAT DOES
THAT MAKE YOU . . . .

The Ones you Marry and the One you Date

For men (*and sometimes women*) operating under the concept that it's ok to pursue those you know you will never take home to mother all while keeping your options open for others you see as being acceptable candidates, are doing not only the lesser valued person a disservice but yourselves as well and what I mean by this is first there is the bad karma issue, with you taking advantage of someone you know is lacking in **someway** (*or who you think is lacking, with you being quick to judge them superficially without taking into consideration all that comprises them; like the person wanting more from life than what they are able to do right now. Remember everybody's journey is different with us all having to get past certain issues in our lives before actually coming into our own, so what you see now may not be what you see later once the person takes the initiative, by making the changes they need to make in order to get where they need to go. (Side note here: I did say them taking the initiative and not you pushing them into something they are not ready for yet, again in situations like this you should only be playing the role of someone who encourages and not one looking to save the person, with them running with the ball from their own motivation; doing anything else is you trying to change them, something relating to the previous section.*)); **with** you feeling because of this gives you the right to do. All of which can put you in the position of reaping what you sow from either you never being able to win the desire of someone who you feel is worth the effort, something happening due to the bad rep you have now garnered with those having any kind of sense not wanting to be bothered with you or you, yourself, not living up to the standards you're set for others, with the person realizing that they could do better elsewhere. Secondly, because you are purposely seeking those you know are only just for the now, with them being seen as nothing in your eyes, you cheat yourself as well as them out of a moment of personal growth with you learning to look beyond the obvious under the understanding that there might be more to this person then what society and upbringing have to say about what deems acceptable; and as far as the intended victim is concerned, possibly being furthered scarred from them continually being treated less than what they should be treated with them again further putting themselves in degraded positions until some kind of revelation comes about allowing them to see their true value with them realizing that they deserve something better. Since we all are flawed in someway, it behooves us to be a little more sympathetic to all we encounter, working off the hope that what we do unto others will be done onto us; because of the impression we don't always know we make on those we desire ourselves, with them also maybe looking at us as just a stepping stone to a much better opportunity. Again remember we are all Yah's children with him loving us all and in saying this he expects us to treat each other with love and respect (*seeing that we are all brothers and sisters in Christ*), so when we take it upon ourselves to think that we have a right to discard a person because of a limited point of view, we are exalting ourselves over Yah, by implying that some of who he created are not up to par (*with us feeling we have a right to condemn them because of it*), something which, to me, is treading in dangerous territory. Not saying that everything is for everybody, but that for everybody there is a somebody and what may not work for you, may work for someone else (*or as what one would consider to be silver is gold to another*). So again when you encounter those who you feel don't fit into your plans, consider politely bypassing, instead of taking advantage of them because of their shortcomings or even what some consider strengths if you are using them just to say you were with them. And again in cases like this, you may only be pursuing someone because of the heighten recognition they bring (*or for the feathering of one's hat*), with you seeing it for just only that, all while desiring someone other than them who you feel is a little more low key (*or less troublesome with them requiring not as much maintenance*) and could see yourself settling down with; something that may be very hurtful to the injured party (*or the pursued person in this example*) with them thinking that what they're bringing to the table guarantees them whatever as well as whoever with them finding out that it really means nothing. (*Where with someone who we consider not to be all that could kind of understand why they would get dissed.*) Either way, the motivation for doing this is the same with you only looking at them as temporary solace. Something else to keep in mind here is you being a possible vessel as well as a friend (*platonic of course and definitely without benefits*) with you again encouraging this person in a positive way if you feel a change in behavior is **needed** (*like them willingly allowing themselves to be exploited or in cases where the person thinks that they are all that, you providing them with a reality check,* (**lovingly of course**) *that the world doesn't revolve around them*) **and** by doing this you are actually playing the role a man should be **playing** (*the kind of man Yah wants you to be with you ministering to them, with you also being an example* (**from your displaying integrity**) *as to what they should be looking for when it* *comes to future romantic endeavors instead of the same ones they keep running into with their only concern being is them getting theirs)* **with** the other person now feeling good about your paths crossing and you feeling good knowing that you added to their life instead of taking away from it by being a blessing to them in someway *(something which again we all are suppose to be)*. I know a lot of guys will probably say that for the most part they do have honest intentions when pursuing members of the female persuasion with them not being able to control the change of direction, something which I agree may all be true, however once you realize that there is nothing to work with here with the person *(or just the situation in general)* turning out to be less than what you expected, is when you should be taking the high road by either again politely moving on or doing the above. Other things relating to this issue are:

a. Wasting others time by blindsiding them under the false hope that this situation may have a chance of blossoming into something long term. And the real shame in this *(other than outside of this person getting hurt)* is while they are putting all their energies into what they think is promising, someone else could be pursuing them who really does appreciate all of what and who they are with them really having honest intentions. *(All saying that you are guilty of blocking someone else's prospects by holding up their show when you already knew that you didn't want anything anyway.)*

b. Fooling yourself into thinking that you are missing out from either false illusions with you working off the belief that the grass is greener on the other side or from others opinions. Here, in the latter you may find yourself discarding a person solely on the basis of those in your inner circle with you allowing their feelings, on what they think is best for you, to take precedence over your own, then once you find out that you were better off where you were, you are now put in the position of having to make amends. In situations like this, as well as the former, is where it becomes imperative that you be settled in your life with you being your own person. Also something else to be aware of here when relying on others' input you value is knowing that in most cases a lot of their advice is usually based on where they are currently at in their own lives, all of which becomes invalid if it doesn't directly apply to your situation; and why you need discernment with you making sure that whatever they are saying really does. (*Example: The person of influence being concern about a person's looks because of them wanting to impress others with you being past things like that. Now in this scenario because the person you chose didn't meet the approval of whoever's putting their two cents in, they express disapproval; so of course now the question here is why would you allow yourself to be suede by this person when you know that between the two of you, you are operating off of different concepts.*)

c. In relation to the false illusion issue with you thinking that you are missing out, another consequence here is when you find out that not only is the grass not greener, but maybe even worst than what you walked away from with the new person having more drama than you anticipated or that what you thought was important really wasn't with your realizing how superficial you were being. Again this point has kind of already been touch on but I thought it should be re-emphasized again because of it being such a common trap we all fall into.

d. Now concerning those you pursue just to say you were with them (*something mentioned earlier in this section*), who you know don't have a chance in (*fill in the blank with whatever works for you here*) of meeting moms. Whether it be the "you can't bring em' home if they can't use momma's comb" ones or those where age differences or internal racial conflicts (*you know like the light skin/ dark skin issue, a very touchy subject where it's widely believed that one is preferred more than the other*) are involved, the reasons behind you choosing them are superficial with you knowing that whatever they bring to the table means very little to those who's approval matters most, with you discarding them once they've served their purpose. And one of the problems with this is because a lot of these people have been built up in such a way where they feel a certain sense of entitlement, makes it hard for them to understand why you would've pulled the rug up from under them; something which you can't blame them for since in most cases, it is usually society's fault with us putting certain people on pedestals because of attributes we deem admirable. Something again which when does happens makes them feel like they are being punished because of it and why their disappointment is greater than others, even to the point where it becomes more difficult for them to bounce back. Remember using people like this is almost as bad as being emotionally abusive with you showing how much of a hater you really are because of you, in your own way, putting someone in the position of second guessing themselves; something all possibly resulting from your own issues.

e. And lastly, you getting hemmed up into a situation where, because, let's say, a pregnancy coming out of it and you not being able to free yourself from someone you see as not having a future with (*another issue that commonly occurs in these kinds of spectacles and that has been brought up several times; with the significance, as well as, consequence being so great that I had to mentioned it again. Because as you should already know the real victim here will probably be the child if you choose not to take responsibility for your actions or come across in a resentful manner from having to*). And even in cases where it is not about a child resulting from it, with you desiring to dismiss the whole experience once you have achieved the goal of getting yours, you can sometimes take the position of it never happening at **all** (*or minimize whatever did so as to make it appear how little it meant to you with it all being because of you wanting to save face with the new person. Which if you become desperate enough can turn really ugly with you resorting to violence just to shut whoever might be able to make trouble for you up. Again all explaining why I'm putting such great emphasis on this particular point with me wanting you to see how deep this can get. Now if the person you are doing this for buys into the foolishness by believing your lies, they are aiding in this feeling of invincibleness you've garnered, with your fall being that much harder when that day comes*). **Something** you hope will allow you to move on with your life on a clean slate. But again like anything else what's done in the dark will always come to light. Which again is why purposely pursuing those who you know already will never make the cut is just plain stupid and very much not worth the headaches you may incur from it when you find yourself having to explain your past actions to others or if the person you so wronged is now in the position of having the upper hand with you being at the mercy of them.

Now of course the bottom line from saying all of this is that we, as humans, all deserved to be loved, something if you can't do, with you wanting to take advantage of someone else's vulnerability for whatever reason (*as well as judging the person when you don't really have the right to do so*), can cost you greatly in the long run. (*Side note: Another issue that needs to be addressed here is about those you choose already being vulnerable. A lot of times women have been exposed to sex at a very young age from things like abuse or them having low self-esteem with them allowing themselves to be used for the sake of getting another's attention (something which in both cases can lead to sexual promiscuousness). So now the question here is if you put someone like your mother, sister, daughter, or any other woman you deeply care for in the same position would you want someone to take advantage of them like that just because they didn't have enough for themselves to not let it happen. Something that may even explain why (if someone like your mother was actually this person) your father might not have wanted to be bothered because of him seeing her as well as all that is connected to her (meaning you) as a nuisance with you both now being a thorn in his side from him originally designating her as the lesser valued person. Just like if your mother thought she could get a better deal elsewhere because of her not seeing worth in your father with her easily discarding him without taking into consideration how it may affect you; like with her new man resenting you because of you being someone else's child and him treating you that way, and it possibly being ok with her because of this as well. With the point again in all of this being that there are consequences when you proceed in these kinds of endeavors under selfish motivations, so again think about it!)*

If the answer to this section's initial statement is something other than a compassionate person with you feeling that everybody merits consideration as well as respect, then what you just read directly applies to you; with you understanding that by feeling that a person is not worthy, and you still allowing them into your space is setting yourself up for being judge by the company you keep as well. Because after all why would a person waste their time with those who are not worth their time unless they, themselves, can relate (or for all you players out there, playing with tainted goods just because you can). Now of course the other explanation could and hopefully would be is that you are aiming to become a better person with you desiring to be enlighten and by doing so may result in a blessing with this now being a dress rehearsal (with it preparing you for the real thing) because when you give regard to what already exist in your life you will no doubt be guaranteed a greater reward later.

Be careful what you ask for
cause you just might get it,
with it being more than you can handle . . . .
For who you are from
do you really know

Part Two, Who you Bring Home What are you Basing it on?

Something relating to not only a few points made earlier in the previous section but from the "Women and the Games We Play" section as well concerning how men, in most cases, base their final decision on whom they choose to settle down with on those who's traits are somewhat similar to that of their mother. Now again for the sake of wanting to make the point about you having an overall understanding on the dynamics of what comprises any one person, you need facts as well as clarity because without either you may be stepping into something that you will certainly not be prepared for. Not trying to imply that you should be scrutinizing those of influence in such a way that you are looking to condemn them however again it is important to remember that we all, as humans, are constant works in progress with us continuingly learning and growing as we go **along** (*all saying that the person you have always had great admiration for could've started out being a stone trip in their younger years but through enlightenment and experience is now nothing less than the calm in the storm with them being held in high regard by others because of it*) **and** without you taking things like this into consideration, when you do set out to find those comparable to them, you could inadvertently discount the fact that though they may represent the essence of those you admire they still may not be completely there yet in terms of maturity, **etc.** (*as well as possibly having to modify a few of your expectations because of changing times with you understanding that what your mom was able to do may not be feasible for any woman of today; an issue touched on earlier*). **Which**

is why this becomes a problem for you from being drawn to someone who you now find yourself in constant conflict with, with you also being completely disillusioned from all the possible baggage, drama or foreign concepts they bring to the relationship; something which gives justification as to why there should be honest communication between our parents and us, with them being totally up front about what actually went down in their lives; and by doing so they provide us with valuable insight about not only what they have learned from their past mistakes but what makes them tic; and from this we can also gain a better understanding of our own inner workings because who we are is not just based on examples that were set before us (*or instruction that was given during our formative years*) but what we've inherited as well with us doing what comes naturally, something once we get a hand on it (*or understand how this behavior creates certain outcomes*) with us coming to terms on the grief it may cause in our lives, can be corrected (*if it's merited*) instead of us having to endure the same foolishness our predecessors endured already from the detours that have been made for us, with us being rerouted in other directions. Now getting back to the subject, without examples or guidance as to what to do (*in regards to how you go about tackling issues that may arise with its impact being possibly key on how it all turns out*) or expect from others, who qualities match up to those we pursue, we can find ourselves in a state of disarray with us completely mishandling things. Whether it be throwing in the towel, something that could always leave us wondering if this person was actually the one (*just not right now though*) or stay with us trying to impose on them things they are not ready for yet with us being exhausted and burned out from it all by the time the light bulb comes on for them, and the residue of a possible dysfunctional reality being left with those created during this relationship. Now of course, one of the best solutions for dealing with this issue, is taking a step back with you first doing some serious soul searching with you finding out where you emotionally stand in this, then once you feel that there is something to work with here, you should start seeking understanding from a spiritual point of view as well as going to the source who you feel may have **answers** (*that is if they are honest enough to come clean about things, instead of discouraging you from knowing what you are about to go up against or are now too much on their high and mighty with them acting as if they were always a saint* (*side note: A lot of times when we bring people home to meet our parents, especially those who are the spitting image of their former selves, they usually try to discourage us from having any further involvement with the person, without taking into consideration that someone took a chance on them, while they too were not at their best* (*with them also forgetting about where they, themselves, could've been if certain opportunities weren't presented to them, a fact we should all keep in mind. Because if they hadn't existed for us who knows where we would have ended up as well.*))) **Now** in cases, where your parents didn't make it through the storm, when this happens, hopefully they'll be able to provide you with a few good words of advice on how to deal with a person like this, something, if it is productive, could benefit you greatly, (*this again of course is outside of spiritual guidance, which is really the best way to go when seeking true enlightenment*) with you now being correctly influenced, instead of operating off of impulsive emotions. And what I mean by this is if you choose to continue this endeavor, with you knowing that there might be a few surprises in store as far as having to deal with behavior you're not accustom to, you still need some kind of reference point, because without it you will only be repeating history again with things going a bust for you as **well.** (*Side note: The difference between knowing the deal before entering into a relationship and walking into it naively under the assumption that all was good between those you admire from the very beginning when it really wasn't is (as it relates to the latter) you having a more difficult time coping with conflicts as they come into play (especially since you are basing everything you know on what you saw with you not being privy to what actually went on); and again because of this you could be left with feelings of failure from you not being able to achieve the same kind of success your predecessors had.*) **On** the other hand if you feel that the situation is definitely not for you with you truly seeing no hope for a future here, move on, but only after gaining some true understanding as to why you are drawn to certain kinds of people, because until you do you will keep running into these same personalities. Something again going back to my original statement about who you bring home and why you are drawn to them? Other things to take into consideration from this are:

a. Trying to changing a person as it relates to inherited traits, as well as generational curses. Again it is important to remember there are many different factors behind what makes up a person with the spiritual connections having just as much impact on who we are as what we are taught. So though we might not have been exposed to certain behavior coming up, still does not mean that it won't manifest itself in someway later.

And as far as curses goes, since this outcome is based on behavior or ideas passed down from others, things will continue with them rejecting any kind of positive **encouragement** (*unless some kind of spiritual revelation occurs with the person involved desiring to change and them being committed to whatever needs to happen in order for this change to come about*). **Something** all saying why you should understand who you are getting involved with because again you can't change anyone just only in the approach you take on how you relate to them. But also as this relates to this particular section, what you are used to is not necessarily always good for you either. And again in saying this when you do run into people who are coming from a better place, you could find yourself pulling away from **them** (*something usually all being either because of your own stupidities or from the egging on by others (namely your mother) who are self serving with them wanting things to stay as they are with them being able to still take advantage of the situation; something again all being based on them looking at you as the surrogate man in their lives and you going along with it because of misguided loyalties*) **with** you desiring to seek out those of a more dysfunctional nature. Something which when does happens recreates the scenario of another dysfunctional relationship, with the possibility of it continuing over and over again. That's why moving outside of your comfort zone, by allowing yourself to be open to those whose concepts are not that of the familiar, can benefit you greatly. And by doing this you get to expand your horizons with you seeing that there is more than just one perspective; something that (*once it becomes clear that certain influences you have been operating under maybe lacking in validity*) could lead you to wanting to seek the truth as to how things should be. Something again going back to what was mentioned earlier about a revelation of some kind occurring in order to bring about change with things like friendship (*something a lot less complicated than you jumping in romantically*) or another's example being the force behind it. (*Side note: Whether it's you or the other person involved being the vessel used in helping to create this change, what a person represents is what motivates another to desire something different, another thing. Also something else to mention as it relates to generational curses, is when they are about to be broken, with the person involved now opening themselves up to new ideas, a struggle from within will possibly occur as they again now start moving away from old concepts and loyalties; something which explains why patience would be necessary when dealing with them.*)

b. Remembering that your mother is a woman too. A point that needs to be made because again of what most men base their choices on whom will become their mates on. Once in your mother's life she was sought out for her curves, sensuality, personality and womanly ways, not just for her future motherly skills or on how great of a wife she might be. And in saying that when you do pursue someone and she behaves in such a way where it's more about having a good time than on wifely virtues how do you know that you are not looking at a mirrored imaged of your mother. I mean you weren't there when your father was courting her, nor do you

know what it was about her that intrigued **him** (*of course,*
unless he is willing to share with him giving you the 411
and even with that you may only be getting the PG version,
because after all we talking about your mother here). **So** the
next time you are quick to judge a woman because
you think that she could never be somebody's wife or
mother, remember before your mother was your mother
she was and maybe still is (*if your parents are currently*
together) your father's wife and/or woman. Which means
whatever she did or is still doing to keep the home
fires burning is what you might be doing right **now**
(*even though you are not suppose to be doing anything if you*
are not married, with the same being for your parents (during
their courting stage) if that was the case for them, but they
did it anyway (getting past any storms they've encountered
from doing things out of orders (or maybe not if things didn't
work out))) **with** it still not having much bearing on the
fact that she is still a great representation of what you
feel a woman should be, with you having the up most
respect for her. (*Side note: In reference to doing things out*
of order, remember there will always be consequences from
these kind of actions, something that could possibly turn into
a generational curse if the parties involved ignore the outcome
with them passing down bad behavior to others (meaning their
offsprings), *with them in turn continuing things under the*
same philosophy (something that could possibly bring about
catastrophic results for those who follow in the footsteps of the
ones who came before them with them being brought to their
knees because of it; an outcome that may need to happen in
order for the cycle to be broken). *That's why those of influence*

learning from their mistakes benefits all concern with them now being able to pass on information that could nip certain behavior in the butt.)

c. Something relating to the previous point is when you misread a situation under the thinking that the person you are pursuing is a great representation of the ideal woman with them not turning out to be that at all from knowing how to play the game in such a way that they were able to pull the wool over your eyes, then once they are able to get you to seal the deal you find out that they really weren't all that interested in being a wife or mother but just to get married. And I say this because as women, most of us have been taught what a lady is and isn't (*or are privy to certain information specifically about you that would help in aiding us in someway*), so it is easy to put on a facade with us giving you what you want instead being who we are. However there are cases where a person doesn't either no better or just chooses to keep it real, with them using sincerity as their weapon of choice to reel you in and because of this a sense of genuineness could be felt with you again knowing that this person will be bringing their best to the table (*that is if you gave the person a chance instead of opting to bypass for so-called better prospects*). So again don't judge a book by it's cover but instead by the depth of the read.

d. Understanding that there is a difference between your mother, as your mom, and her as a woman becomes important when pursuing romantic endeavors. And what I mean by this is though your partner should be someone you can depend on for love and support, the ideal (*whether it be yours or hers*) of them becoming the now mother figure in your life should not be an option. Something which when you do understand this, will have bearing on qualities that really should have merit when dating someone in the first place; like with you being more concerned with the person's true desire to be a wife and mother. Then once she becomes your wife, you allowing her to come into the role on her own terms instead of you constantly comparing her to someone else's standards (*with whatever way your mother does what she does being hers and your wife's way being hers with you appreciating them both*). All of which is the problem because in most cases the roles are blurred, with you choosing women who act more like your mother than them just being a partner with you being treated like a child because of this and them now both competing for the top spot with you being caught in the middle. Something that has no merit because of the kind of emotional and physical bond that already exist between a mother and her child (*remember she carried you for nine months, fed and cared for you, until you were able to stand on your on two feet, and will love you unconditionally forever*). Where as your wife though being your partner and possibly mother of your children, is not your parent but someone you chose to spend the rest of your life with, based on the love you have for her (*a changing variable*). So now again how can the two compete and more importantly why are they allowed to. Not trying to say that there is something wrong with desiring certain attributes that remind you of your mother, especially since being a wife is not just about tending to your romantic needs, but also caring for your children as well as the home you have together (*if applicable, with her not working*). However with the latter usually being all you see growing up (*with you not being privy to pretty much nothing else*) you can find yourself drawn to women like this with you now having to deal with two opposing forces clashing over who is what to who and of course you now having to choose; something that could have been avoided if you'd just put your foot down with you explaining to both why they need to stay in their respective lanes instead of the two continually seeing each other as a **threat** (*with your wife learning that without your upbringing you wouldn't be the man that you are now (something probably all having to do with why you two are together) and your mother understanding that through the love and support of your wife the process of your growth as one continues.*) **Something** else to be considered here that was touched on earlier in a previous section is if your wife does appreciate you as a man then she should have no problem showing reverence to those who are responsible for what you have **become** (*something that if she doesn't see as being all that great, says very little about her since she proceeded in marrying you anyway*), **with** her looking to the source for a few words of wisdom from time to time (*as it relates to your offsprings*), just like in the same way your mother shouldn't have a problem taking a step back with her playing a supporting role and not an overseer, because after all she had an opportunity to be the woman of the house with her finding her way so it is only fair that she give your wife a chance to do the same instead of spending all her time reminding your wife what she is lacking in. Also, in reference to those you choose who want to play your mother, establishing boundaries earlier on may deter a person's desire to do this, however the problem though here is that in most cases the person's motivation behind doing this is more about them having control than them just not knowing better which means she really is not all that interested in wanting to be corrected; with her moving on if she feels she can achieve greater success somewhere else (*all of which saying why it becomes necessary that you check her in the initial stages of the relationship because the sooner you find out what is really behind the behavior the better thereby giving you the opportunity to cut your losses before things get too deep*).

e. Another issue touched on earlier concerns you being drawn to people who are the essence of those you admire and changing times with the question being what would your mother look like today. Now the reason for putting any kind of energy into this point at all is because of both parties needing to understand the impact progress has on perspective with priorities being greatly affected by it. And what I mean by this is because of the limited opportunities available to our mothers back in the day, what she was delegated to was nothing except to be a stay at home wife and **mother** (*or in some rare cases a lesser valued occupation with her still having to hold down the fort in such a way that she did it all with her being looked upon* *as being some kind of superwoman because of it; something today's woman would never happily sign up for with a lot of us balking at it if expected to because of realistic sensibilities).* **However**, with us now being encouraged to be all we can be, redefines what a woman is and because of this things relating to domestic issues are put on the back burner with career endeavors taking it's place; so again who's to say the path our elders would have chosen if given the same opportunity. With again the point being made about you being drawn to the essence of who they are and why taking things like this into consideration when mulling over on whether or not you should move forward with a relationship becomes important with you having to adjust your thought processes on how you think things should play out, especially if she opts not to be a traditional wife with her wanting you pick up the slack in the neglected areas. Something being the same for us, with us *(meaning women)* understanding that to much is given, much is required; something again from which we also have to understand that we can't expect you to carry the ball like in the past with us now having to pick up the financial **slack**, *(cause after all if you are expected to help out domestically, then why not; something else also saying that we don't have a right to complain about you not being like our daddies with us knowing as a man you may not necessarily have the same opportunities that were afforded him).* **And** from this last point, another issue of concern here is since you are now no longer necessarily the breadwinner anymore or *(as it relates to Black men)* have the same kind of support systems that encourage you to move ahead like we now do, we are forced to adjust our thought processes even further with us trying to balance out our roles by making sure that you don't feel like you are now being emasculated with you feeling the need to regain your position by doing whatever it takes (*from other things like dominance or unscrupulous means*). Being drawn to men who (*just like you as it relates to your mother*) have similar qualities to that of our fathers, we fall into the same trap with us becoming disillusioned from the realization that though there is a reason for why we are drawn to each other, because of changing times what we see now may be a far cry from what we are use to; with the real problem being here is (*as it relates to both parties*) that neither one has ever considered working off of where the person is currently at (*with both roles being clearly defined*) but instead off of something no longer viable.

f. Lastly, for men who had no mother figure (*or were raised by an elder in the family*) in their life, because of you not having a reference point to go on at all or the one you had was so far off the map (*meaning too generationally un-relatable*) to have ever been considered a valid one, you could inadvertently find yourselves seeking those who provide that missing ingredient. Something that can cause you to digress when it comes time to stepping up like a man should or you really never being able to truly commit because of resentment you bring to the relationship (*because of your general feelings about woman with you not trusting them*). Now again, in cases like this, some spiritual counseling is required with you first getting healed from not having your mother in your life. And from this you should be able to move forward in a more positive way with you making better choices.

Some of the reasons behind issues like these are from us pursuing romantic endeavors before we have truly define ourselves with us moving from being under the thumb of our parents to that of others without doing a stare and compare first. Not taking the time to see what life has to offer with us never emotionally leaving the nest, limits our **growth** (*something once we begin to feel trapped (from the realization that we've married someone reminiscing of our parents) could lead us to resorting to unscrupulous measures as a way of coping with the situation*). **Another** reason for our lack of clarity (*something again touched on earlier*) is when our parents choose not to share by withholding information about some of their past (*es*) sexcapades. Though there are many different ways Yah shows us that he is Yah, it's important to understand that the storms he allows us to go through with him making a way out for us are not just for our benefit but for others as well with them knowing that we all have crosses to bear. So when we try to put on airs that all was perfect in our world we are cheating those who may need reassurance of some kind that they too are not alone with us giving them hope that things can also work out for them. Something else to consider here is when those who, them themselves have suffered slights (*with them in turn inflicting pain on others*) see the ones they've victimized make a better life for themselves, forces them to take a step back with them realizing that if they had chosen a different path instead of waddling in their own self-pity they too might've escaped the trapping of their negative surroundings (*or circumstances*) with them eventually deciding to turn over a new leaf because of it. Again something all being the power of showing one scars with you not being ashamed of what did happen in your life with you again understanding why you should be counting it all joy because of what you have now gained from it. Think of people who were born with afflictions, whether it be life threatening illnesses, physical impairments, or even emotional issues (*thing we all could suffer from with it happening to anyone of us later in life*) and how they still find ways to inspire others by living full lives (*that is if the people around them, who say they have their best interest at heart allow them to*); that's why I believe people in situations like this are here, with Yah saying to us if he brought someone into the world in such a way that to us we see as suffering and them still being able to achieve and be all they can be then what excuse would we have if we found ourselves in the same predicament with the only choice being but to follow suit. And that's really the point since we all are born of sin we come into the world having to get past something so reference points become important for all to have and why they exist.

How Double Standards Can Hurt You and Don't Ask What You Can't Afford to Lose

There's an old saying that goes "Do as I say (*or what I want you to do*), not as I do (*with you not judging me for the same thing*), something in this day and time you'd think no longer applies. However as another saying goes, "The more things change the more they stay the same" with men feeling that they have liberty to do whatever, desiring women to stay in their place while they wait for you to grow up or to just put up with your foolishness, because well I mean after all boys will boys and shouldn't be expected to adhere to the same rules they dish out to everyone else. Something again that makes absolutely no sense, since we are all judged by the same Yah with no one being given a pass for their transgressions over anybody else (*because remember even in the stories of David, Moses, etc. when they screwed up they felt his raft* (*with love of course*) *something being the same for us*). Besides since you are expected to be the leaders in our homes and communities, then it would be reasonable to assume that you'd be leading by example and not by the agenda you have, meaning whatever you expect from us you should already be doing, with you understanding when a foundation is shaky whatever is resting on it will likely be affected by its instability (*or you not being right makes whoever depends on you being greatly impacted by your actions*). And even if you don't see it that way (*with you not feeling a sense of duty to others*) think about it from this standpoint, when it all comes crashing down guess who it's going to fall on (you) with you losing everything you worked so hard for (*like reputation, admiration, position, etc.*), an outcome that could leave you empty (*from your now defunct support system you decided to abandon earlier because of your lack of regard for them while you were doing your dirt*) with you suffering regret from it, especially once you realize that the stance you took really wasn't worth it. Another problem with this here is a sense of arrogance you exhibit under the thinking that you are not obligated to return the favor, like as if the other person is suppose to keep giving and giving without the benefit of return of **investment** (*now*

when I say this I am talking about romantic ventures not basic human interaction (something where it doesn't matter if you see a return of investment) with Yah giving us definite directives to follow, like for women with us respecting the position of headship you've been given in the home and you loving us as Christ loved the church with you embracing and caring for us in the same way he does his flock (or his children). Something which again when doesn't happen renders a relationship vulnerable with it eventually falling apart. Because of the lack of integrity and consideration in this kind of behavior is why the "Do as I say, not as I say" theory never flies. And even more so when you feel justified in doing things like this from carrying the ball (or the weight of responsibility) an action that merits a reminder from Yah that it is only through him that all blessing flow and through him they will cease if he becomes displeased by how you choose to live your life).
Examples coming out of this:

   a. The "me a ho I don't think so" philosophy is one of man's greatest offense, with you feeling that you can sleep around all day long with whomever and still coming off in a positive light, something the same not being afforded to women, with us being penalized for it. Now please tell me why you don't you see a problem with this, especially since anyone other than our mate is considered off limits! Again women are not here just for your disposal with you feeling that you can go through them like water, but human beings not to be taken advantage of even when they put themselves in the position to (*and I say this in the same way I know how we are suppose to see you as well, so I'm not letting us off the hook either, but this is about you so . . .*). And again one of the problems with this is when you find yourself having to explain your actions later to the person you see as being the love of your life (*or because of your reputation being on the line as it relates to you wanting to be seen by others as a person of good character*) you now want to play down these past sexcapades with you attempting to act as if it never happened (*or that it meant very little to you when you did*); a situation that could make you look not as much of a gentleman (*at least in our eyes*) with you showing your lack of respect for us in general (*something that could eventually lead a person to feeling insecure about how you may view them one day if things go a bust*). Remember no woman in her RIGHT mind is going to accept you sowing your oats with her being limited by your unrealistic expectations. If you want a virtuous woman, then you need to be a virtuous man. And if it is too late to be the case, then all I can say to you is to treat this person in the same manner in which you want to be treated by moving forward without bringing whatever happened in their past into the relationship (*and again being one of the consequences of dating*). Another issue coming out of this is, because in most of these scenarios, you have already decided who you think is ok to play **with** (*something you're not authorized to do with you designating them as the lesser valued person; something again saying very little about you with it shedding light on the kind of person you really are from the company you keep*) **and** who you consider to be girlfriend or wife material, you create animosity between these women with the one who feels slighted desiring to mess up your story once you decide to give her (or them) the boot and the one, who you hold in high regard, wanting in turn to get you back by returning the favor with her stepping out on you. With feelings of betrayal being behind both their motives after realizing they've been duped in someway like of course the one you've been playing with just being something to do for the moment and other one who was considered the one not being only humiliated, from knowing that there were others, but for possibly being underestimated (*or reduced down to just a showpiece*) with you not looking at her as someone who could've been all the woman you needed with her feeling less than one because of it; (*something explaining why she would again now need validation of some kind*).

b. Something else relating to the previous section is your past (*or what you are still currently doing*) coming back to haunt you in the form of what your offsprings bring home. For the most part a lot of men only live for the moment with them not really putting a lot of thought into the future impact of their actions (*like again reputation or bad karma*). And since most people desire to move on with their lives, they attempt to reinvent themselves; something done for the purpose of wanting to come across as being more innocence than they really were, which means whatever dirt they created they now want swept under the rug. Then once the inevitable happens, with one of their love ones bringing home someone of a similar nature, they start to trip from them now seeing remnants of their former self standing before them. And in cases where you are still out there doing your thing, your anxiety becomes that much more heighten; something I'd hope would cause you to finally wake up with you now understanding why you need to be a better example, with you also understanding that you can't expect others to treat the ones you cherish any better than how you treat those you pursued. Also here when the truth eventually comes out about you not necessarily being all that upstanding you will now be left with having to make amends to all those you let down with the relationship possibly being permanently broken.

c. Having unrealistic expectations, with you judging others for things that you, yourself fall short of (*like weight issues, you not being where you should be, etc.*); something that once the other person catches on to, puts you in the position of being judged even more harshly, especially if the person you are involved with was the subject of ridicule with them now being on their A game; something in either case could cause them to move on to someone better. Another thing from this is to a lot of people this behavior comes off as a form of emotional abuse with you being overly critical of a person with them not being able to do the same by pointing out your flaws; something that could lead to major upheaval when they finally decide that they've had enough. (*Side note: Two of the best examples of this is when you target a woman just on the basis of her looks alone, with you becoming defensive when she expects you to be a person of means (or deep pockets); remember if you want to be desired for the person you are and not only for your assets alone then you should be approaching us under the same motivation otherwise we have just as much right to be as superficial as you are (as you now would be attracting the energy you put out) with you understanding why you should be ok with our "Ain't Nothing Going on But the Rent" stance instead of labeling us as gold-diggers; something giving credence as to why you need to be getting your act together in the first place before pursuing romantic ventures. Now with the other example here is when you choose to pursue those without children with you not only having them but along with this extra baggage comes baby momma drama as well; something explaining why you choose not to be bothered with those who do (with you not having to deal with the same issues or just on the basis of knowing that the father is still part of picture, something again saying how one sided this situation really is since the woman you are involved with has to deal with your children's mother presence. Also relating to this is the time and energy you desire of others to put into the relationship with you not being able to do same because of your obligations to your children). Of course the obvious problem with this is your putting another person in a position you, yourself don't want to be in; something most would consider to be pretty hypocritical on your part with you wanting them to endure drama not of theirs. Another problem with this is the unfinished business you should've handled before moving on to another relationship, with you using your lackings (or fear of confrontations) as an excuse for not stepping up like a man, with you still allowing your children's mother to continue running the show. Something all of which could cause you loss if the person you are now involved with becomes weary from being caught in the middle of this mess, and even more so if she is constantly pitted against the mother with you wavering between the two. Again you can't ask something of someone your not willing to do yourself with the question being then, why are you).*

d. Something relating to point c, is you cheating yourself out of meeting someone who could be possibly more compatible, because of you chasing after those who may be out of your league. And what I mean by this is when a sense of entitlement occupies your spirit with you feeing that you deserve something you, yourself can't deliver (*or be*) you overlook those who may be better suited for you, with it usually taking a negative outcome occurring (*like you getting dumped over and over again, or you finally being honest with yourself from the revelation that you just can't keep up*) in order for you to see the light. When we approach things in this manner it is usually the result of our own insecurities with us looking to be elevated through those we associate with; with the only real solution being you loving yourself as well as finding your way. Then once you become more situated (*learning now to be comfortable in your own skin*) you will start to seek out those who are a much better fit. (*Side note: Again there is nothing wrong with having higher aspirations (with you desiring those who compliment you) but until things fall into place with you achieving your goals you will be caught in the "in between two worlds" zone; something that could cause you to use people who you see as just for the moment or experiencing the subject at hand with you getting dumped by someone who feels that you are not moving fast enough for their taste. With the best advice being you staying neutral by just maintaining platonic friendships until you have finally arrived with it then being ok to pursue those you feel now are on the same page as you.)*

Understanding that in order for any relationship to survive, the rule of fair play has to be incorporated into it; with both parties working together as a unit and not individuals looking for self gain or being able to exalt themselves over others for the purpose of maintaining the status quo with them continuing to live their lives as they please without taking the needs of those involved into consideration; something being the true motivation behind the "Do as I say, not as I do" philosophy with you seeking out those you feel will allow you to get away with this either through dominance or by what you have done for them under the thinking that they'll accept your transgressions if the truth ever comes out. All of which is selfish as well as destructive, with the point being made again that no one is above judgment, with how you treat others definitely coming back to haunt you in the form of how you *(or those you hold dear)* will be treated in the future.

Chapter Four

Black Men Issues Continued The Problem with Men is Sex

To all You Singles out there Who Feel That it's
Ok to get Your Groove On
This is a public service announcement
WITH YOU KNOWING WHY YOU SHOULDN'T BE......

Caring whether they stick around or
not cause if it was that important to you
then I guess somebody should've put a ring on it first huh . . . .

Tripping over past sexcapades
From how many there were,
who it was,
and what went down,
something which really shouldn't be of no concern to you . . . .

Getting bent out of shape just because
of you getting caught (or caught up),
with you understanding
that when play you pay . . . .

Introduction

His voice:
The time has come for us to become one
With a no longer contained desire that burns inside of me,
lady of my life come lay, so all that is waiting will be satisfied

Her voice:
My love I would, but am hesitant
Because though the words u say
Bring about a sensual, soothing warmth
they also, bring about a harsh reality
Leading me to ask
If we lay,
Is tomorrow guaranteed or will this moment of ecstasy become just
another empty memory

His voice:
I cannot lie, for I cannot promise what I do not know

Her voice:
Then nigga naw then

(reaching for her hand, he responds)

His voice:
With a no longer contained desire that burns inside of me,
lady of my life, come, take my hand

(pulling back, she responds, saying)

Her voice:
Hesitant, again I ask
If we lay,
Is what that may be created, have us both or will it live wondering why its existence is so damning, feeling the rejection of not being wanted because it was not part the plan

His voice:
I cannot lie, for I cannot promise, what I'm am not prepared for

Her voice:
Then nigga naw then

(reaching for her hand, he responds)

His voice:
With a no longer contained desire that burns inside of me,
lady of my life, come, take my hand

Her voice:
Hesitant, again I ask
If we lay,
When after our bodies have come together, will what u leave behind become an uninvited guest, causing me not only regret but possibly even death

His voice:
I cannot lie, for the consequences of my past have not been tried

Her voice:
Then nigga naw then

(with great emotion, he reaches for her hand)

His voice:
With a no longer contained desire that burns inside of me,
lady of my life, I plead, come take my hand

(pulling away as he starts to take her hand, they overlap in verse with her saying)

Her voice:
Seeing with all that's been said, how can I be expected to give myself to someone who only seems to live for today, someone who has no sense of responsibility or understands that without assurance their words mean nothing
Because without certainty of substance neither of us will prosper from a night of passion that may only be for a night
Even if it lasts a small while, there will always be a sense of shame
For if we lay, I know, there will be no one else but me to blame
Because without a true union of permanence where love, respect, and trust breathe, I've chosen to be a pawn in a fool's game

(his hand now withdrawn, he stands there with his head hanging down)

Ok here we go, all the issues I can think of

The poem before this text expresses pretty much the general sentiment of this particular section with everything discussed thus far leading up to the grand finale "The Problem with Men is Sex and all the Things it cost you When You put too much Emphasis on it". Now I'm sure you can't wait to hear what I have to say on this and believe me when I say that I can't wait to give you an ear full either. Originally the book I really wanted to write was on this subject and this subject alone because well when I sit back and observe (*scratching my head of course*) wondering as to why you do what you do it's easy to see what's really behind the foolishness; I mean from all the deceit, compromising, ambitions, how you treat others, etc. it again all seems to stem from the motivation of being able to bag as many as you can, who you can, and the end result of things when you do; even in cases where love is involved, the same reasoning and/or methodology still applies (*I guess if you don't know any better you work with whatever tools are already available to you*). And the real shame in this is that outside of the act of procreation and physical expression of love that is only suppose to be going on between those who are married with both fully understanding the vows they've taken, sex is something the rest of us need not be concern about; plain and simple so then what is all the hoopla over? A question explaining what the problem really is here, which is you being out of order, with you discarding directives, us, and consequences all for the sake of satisfying ones own flesh and because of this you now constantly crave something you should never have ever even experienced yet, doing anything and everything for it with again everything you incur relating to it. Another sad aspect of this is the fact that you know this already, because if you didn't rules like "those you date and those you marry" wouldn't exist, with you being able to differentiate between those you consider to be ho'es (*or the proper way of saying it whores, man I hate that word*) with you feeling that you have the right to take liberty because of it (*meaning if you see certain women as such with them readily available to you then why not have your way with them*) and those who are **not.** (*Side note: Something else to think about here is how similar a drug user's behavior is to that of a sexual abuser (a label, if you are not already aware of, is not just for molesters or rapists but those indulging in premarital sex) with you taking something that was meant for one purpose with it being exploded for your own personal pleasures. And by doing so you now have a never ending thirst (or what some would see as being a perverted desired) for something that could eventually ruin your life (from things like affairs, unsatisfying romantic ventures, obsessive and degrading behavior, heartache, unwanted responsibilities, and even death) if you don't get a hand on it, something requiring a cleansing of outlook with you not only respecting the original purpose of sex (something in the same way the use of drugs should be respected with us again seeing them as being an integrate part of the physical healing process) but women in general with you understanding that we weren't meant to be objectified. Now the difference between those who have honest intentions with love usually being attached to the act and those who just want to sow their oats, as it relates to the latter, is you purposely seeking out women who you feel you can dupe knowing that the affections you express are only temporary, with you moving on to the next conquest after having your fill of the current one then once you get to a point where you are tire of* *bedding everything in sight (or have come across a woman who totally blows your mind) is when you decide to grow up with you finally desiring to do the right thing (or giving the appearance of wanting to do so, if you already know that your appetite won't be totally satisfied from being monogamous), something completely different than the former where here even though you really are truly interested in seeking real commitment, because of you not following the rules, you could possibly find yourself vulnerable to hurt, disillusionment and/or obligation if you don't immediately meet the one (from dating with you having to go through all the trial and error), something which in either case could bring about another set of problems you could bring about another set of problems you never counted on happening; with it again also saying why, outside of bad karma, in the latter example you're less likely to be disappointed, with you being realistic from understanding the game a little more; however even with this though you still risk a greater consequence occurring when it all falls apart. Something again all saying that in the long run under both circumstances it's just better to do the right thing. Other issues relating to this drug/sexual abuse comparison is how now boundaries become obscure with you seeing everything as fair game, just like in the same way a drug addict does with whatever is available to them becoming a means to an end when they need a fix; or how society also pays for these transgressions because of things like irresponsibility, with us having to pick up the emotional (from resentment), physical (because of abandonment), and financial (too self—absorb or broken) slack of the troubled person where their families are concerned, with them either not in the position of being able to or just choosing not to.)))* **Of** course a lot of men would argue that since I am not a man then how can I begin to understand the depths of their physical needs, something I agree to be very much true because in reality I don't, but what

I do know is that if Yah never puts more on us than we can bear with him directing us to keep ourselves until marriage then where there is a will there has got to be a way. And this goes back to why you need to have that relationship with him first because with it you gain understanding, and from understanding grows into appreciation for his word and through appreciation brings about a desire to obey with discipline following. Something else that needs to be addressed here, is because of man's changing the game through progress and dating customs, we've actually created more problems for ourselves where now instead of a person being able to start their adult life right out of high school or in some cases a little earlier (*like around the age of sixteen or seventeen*) with them being able to find the kind of employment that would've allow them to take on responsibilities like that of a family at that particular time, they now have to postpone things til their mid twenties and beyond (*that's possibly over a six year delay, right*); something creating a major conflict with puberty because like I said earlier, puberty didn't stop because we decided to push things out by broadening our horizons. Not saying that I'm totally against us progressively moving forward or allowing a person the opportunity to come into their own, because stifling growth does nothing for society with us just standing still when we do, however though again with these changes taking place shouldn't there also have been a change in ideology coming into play somewhere with some kind of rework on how to deal with raging hormones being factored in instead of us still being encouraged to continue working off the business as usual" **philosophy** (*something where big business; government, educational institutions and parents all needed to have* *been working together with them formulating a plan of action*); **something** again causing all the sexual chaos we have now, with us moving further and further away from values and morals. Something not just relating to sex, but on our outlook on life as a whole itself with us feeling that we are owed something with the "to much is given much is required" stance no longer applying, something now being replaced with the "I want something for nothing or It's all about me" stance; also since nobody is interested in taking responsibility for their actions anymore we now feel justified bulldozing over whatever is seen as an obstacle. And with you as men not setting the proper examples (*because again of your lack of regard for others*) puts women in the position of following suit with us doing whatever it takes to get where we have to go as well. Whether it be using our womanly charms to manipulate you in someway, something that could easily lead to entrapment; aggression with us stripping you of your manhood; or just bypassing you altogether with us going to the other side or not being bothered at all, again something leaving you just plain out of **luck**. (*Side note: Something relating more to women than you here, is us taking things into our own hands with us using sex as our weapon of choice by making it the focal point of the relationship, an outcome resulting in you not being able to see us as a whole person* (*something being just as much your fault as ours with you being overly consumed with what goes on in the bedroom instead of giving other qualities greater consideration and by doing so with you basing your decision to commit primarily on the sexual aspect of the relationship is why you come up short with you now seeing things clearly from understanding that it takes more than sex to keep the home fires burning*). And with there being so much temptation in the world for *you to fall into if what's at home is nothing more than what you can get out in the streets then it becomes understandable why you'd give in to it, however if we as women bring other things to the table that you can learn to value, especially before we become intimately acquainted with each other with whatever we bring being the main motivation behind you taking that leap, then when others do come your way offering up a little something, something, you as a man now have ammunition to work off of with you knowing that what you have at home is something worth preserving. Another reason why we as women should not be basing you being there on just what goes in the bedroom by saying stupid things like "I'm who you are sleeping with" cause if that's all we've got going for ourselves, well all I can say is, huh; something again being the same for men with you throwing up in our faces what you can do for us financially without realizing that if there is a better deal somewhere else waiting for us we just might take it especially if that's too all you're bringing.)* **Other** things to consider here are a few points already mentioned but unfortunately ole so fitting as it relates to this particular subject, where additional insightful tidbits have been added:

a. Something I said would be discussed throughout this text is the importance of being platonic friends first before moving forward with ANYTHING. Now again of course the obvious advantage in starting out like this is you not getting roped into something with you making sure that this is the right situation for you. And as it relates to this subject, by having a deep emotional bond first creates the ultimate physical one where you now both are truly able to let your guard down because of the kind of trust you've garnered from not jumping into things too soon. Also by removing the physical aspect from the relationship (*with you just seeing the person as a person instead of a sexual object*) allows you to put the focus more on how you relate to each other out of the sheets, something leading into point (b).

b. Continuing from point (a) is the "seeing one clearly from not being blinded by lust" factor. Something considered one of the primary reasons why relationships fail with you getting so caught up in the physical aspect of things (*with again you basing pretty much everything on it*) that you never get past it until you're forced to come to terms with what you have gotten yourself into with all the things that weren't important during the pursuit now being important after the conquest. Now of course one of the problems with intimacy before marriage is that instead of it being part of the glue that helps keep the relationship together it becomes one of the key elements in relational(ship) deception (*with it being used as something of a distraction*) with you not noticing the person's deficiencies. And even in cases where you are clearly aware of them because of the addictiveness of sex you could find yourself having a hard time pulling away, something that could lead to disastrous results with priorities being turned around, as well as dissention being created between your other alliances (*like family and friends*) especially if you feel that they might be working against you by not being supportive with them expressing concern over things they see as a problem. Another issue relating to lust is in order to pull off being casual without feeling guilty about it is turning sex into a necessary **evil** (*something justifying your desire to quench your thirst for it as you please*) with you looking at us (*as well as others like children, animals, etc., I mean I'm just saying it's getting kind of crazy out here*) **as** something to use for the purpose of satisfying it. And because of this it becomes impractical to fall for every person you encounter (*remember J Lo with her marrying, or trying to, every man she had a relationship with*) with the more you see women in this way, the more tainted your outlook becomes with you now totally disrespecting us; something which is one of the end results of doing things out of order with your concepts about relationships and sex now being distorted. Something which again is the real issue here and why there is such a great divide between men and women from seeing each other as a means to an end and nothing more with neither having any regard for the other. Something again that can only be corrected through a wake up call from desiring to be a better person as well as for a more ideal relationship. (*A perfect example of this is one of Hip Hop's a renowned DJ's constantly getting caught with not only female prostitutes but males as well. Defending this freak-etish, he claims not to be neither gay or bi-sexual but just preferably having no preference on who's down there as long as the service they provide is good.*)

c. Guilt got you by the balls, huh. And just like the line suggest is how you get caught up because of the person you are now involved with being able to make you feel guilty from wanting to move on, after having your way with them. Though in most cases both parties are willing participants, somehow the responsibility is still placed on your **shoulders** (*from you not only being the pursuer but also because of your being considered the one who sets the tone with us usually following your lead*) **because** after all women have to be emotionally connected to be intimate; something not being necessarily the same for men in general. So of course that means you would've had to have said or done something on a grand scale to get us in bed otherwise it would not have happened **right** (*of course again even in cases where we are the pursuers here, we're still able to turn the tables on you in such a way that you come out being the bad guy; a question only you can answer as to how*). **With** the longer the farce continuing the more led on we feel. Now it's important to remember that though we are no longer living in the dark ages with the sexual revolution going on since the sixties, men and women still play by different rules with you understanding what being casual really is and us only until WE decide that we want to take things to the next level; something again you are not always necessarily aware of until you decide that you are ready to go on your merry little way and then that's when we play the guilt trip card with us making you feel that you have taken advantage of our **virtue** (*something that usually works because even though you knew you were wrong you still thought you could slide by if things didn't work out*). **And** like with every point being made here if you had never went there (*with it just being for the sake of getting your groove on*) with you operating under the thinking that since everybody else is doing it why can't I or even if you had honest intentions initially and things just didn't gel for you the way you'd have liked, you could have avoided this by not doing anything until things were the way they're suppose to be (*like after you walked down the aisle*) with it being based on definites instead of maybes. Not to say that if you know this is the wrong situation for you that you should feel obligated to stay because of it, it's just that since you did go there you now have to deal with the consequences of doing so by again attempting to handle things as delicately as possible (*I mean it is only the gentlemanly thing to do*) by apologizing to her for wasting her time; something that could lead to you becoming friends. Now of course if she is a sore loser, manipulative, or just out of touch with reality you may need to take a hard stand with you letting the chips fall where they may. In cases like this a lesson will hopefully be learned here where you both understand the importance of (you) not trying to get over and (both) not taking short cuts just to achieve the goal of getting to the finish line of love. Something else to keep in mind here is because most women have been raised on the "Why buy the cow when you can get the milk for free" philosophy with it haunting us in a major way (*from choosing to ignore it*) is why we really don't feel comfortable being in intimate relationships (*for any great length of time*) without some kind of indication that a true commitment is around the corner; something causing us to in turn put pressure on you to make an honest woman out of us and again why thinking twice before pursuing these kinds of relationships would serve you **well** (*because when choose to jump in with both feet by doing it anyway is when the games begin with you now being forced into something that you may not be ready for yet and from that you have again now been cheated out of really properly getting to know this person before taking the leap*) **with** you only considering doing it when you are ready to marry this person because until you put a ring on it you are still working off a maybe with things changing at any given time.

d. Not getting any satisfaction because of all the different experiences you've encountered. And because of this you could find yourself comparing others to your mate. Now the biggest problem with this is you constantly bringing past lovers into your bedroom, expecting similar **results** (*that is if it was good of course, and if it wasn't, well lets just say this creates a whole new set of problems with you desperately feeling the need to find out if your potential lover is sexually compatible to you with them again being put on the spot by having to deliver*). **Something** you just shouldn't be doing with you now dealing with someone new, and not those you're comparing them to. Again one of the pitfalls of intimacy outside of marriage is having too much information to go on and because of this we can put **others** (*or ourselves if the tables are turned with us now being compared to their ex lovers*) **on** the spot with us desiring them to live up to someone else's glory. Remember you were already wrong for being out there like this in the first place so now if you find yourself frustrated because your partner is either not up to par or just may be not as adventurous as someone else would have been then your only recourse is to suck it **up** (*or sever ties (from divorcing) with you going back to whomever you feel can knock it out park the way you want with you getting past whatever you thought they lacked in; something that will definitely bring about severe consequences but hey that's the breaks huh, when the primary focus in the relationship for you is just sex*) **by** first admitting to yourself that you were wrong (*with you allowing Yah to work on you*) then afterwards making a conscious effort to leave the past behind with you really working on creating a healthy sexual relationship based on where this person is currently (*something that might even bring you two closer together because of whatever happening from this point now being based on just you as a couple*).

e. Now part two of point (d) is "If it was so great then why are you here now" issue. And what I mean by this is since mature people know that the majority of lasting relationships are more about than just how good the sex is they try to choose those who meet their needs in a more well rounded way; with them also knowing that certain things are just works in progress, with it all eventually getting better with **time** (*something that has a better chance of being achieve when things like patience, consideration, and good communication are incorporated into the solution*). **However** because of the various outside experiences lurking in the back of our minds, when we are with our mates and things get a little dead in the bedroom we sometimes forget why we chose this person in the first place with us desiring a past (*or maybe something new*) that was and/or is only 20% good instead of being content with something you consider to be 80% alright now (*yeah I listen to TD Jakes too*); something leading to disillusionment with us seeking out something we will eventually come to realize is ever so lacking in everything else with it again all saying why we need to chuck the past, leaving it behind because if it was all that great then why are you with something new **now**. (*Side note: And even if the person who you are still reminiscing about was the one responsible for breaking your heart (with you feeling that no one could ever replace her) you still have to come to terms with the fact that unless you can ride things out solo with you living off the memories of a no longer existing love affair (or failed marriage) for the rest of your life then you have no other choice but to move on; because without realizing it the new person in your life could be someone Yah sent to you, someone who obviously wants to be with you otherwise they would not be there, right? (something that should garner appreciation even more so than what you are mourning over with the above mentioned drama being avoided when you do) And if they are just something to kill the time (with this just being a rebound situation) you are not only hurting yourself (by again possibly putting yourself in the position of getting caught up from desiring to move on once they have served their purpose) but them as well with her being cheated out of finding a person who may really desire something solid (something again also saying why you need to be completely healed before pursuing other romantic ventures because right now you are only looking to fill a void; with it also applying to situations where you are vulnerable as well with you being so distraught that you (from overlooking a* person's negative qualities) could find yourself walking blindly into something that one day bites you in the butt). Now one of the main points that comes out of this issue as well as (d), is when you find yourself in predicaments like this (from having all these different experiences) every person you encounter becomes a soul tie with you now eternally connected to them in someway, something leaving you with memories of regret (with you knowing that you took what was sacred and turned into something frivolous by bedding all these women, something taking away from what was just suppose to be between you and your mate; and because of this, you create another whole new set of problems with you now constantly having to avoid any association with the past (something again most likely born out of your significant other's own insecurities) something that may not be all that feasible when things like social gatherings (or even employment and/or networking opportunities) come up where the person may also be invited, as it relates to the former or involved with as it relates to the latter) and if not regret you looking at the person in a degrading way with you putting your mate on a pedestal (or over compensating with you working off the hope that some of their feelings of inadequacy will eventually be alleviated) in order to justify your actions, because I'm sure in your mind it really doesn't make a whole lot of sense to continue being beholden to someone you are no longer involved with even though you still are with you not being able to shake them otherwise there'd be no reason to bring the subject up (something again that goes back to the philosophy that men have with them designating certain women to being those they just date (with them dropping it like it's hot the way they wanted them to, something you value until you *decide to settle down) and others they consider wife material. Again the problem being with this situation is because your choice is more about appearance (or receiving the approval of others) than on things that make up a truly harmonious and loving relationship (like compatibility, friendship, etc.) you could find yourself looking back at those who you did share these qualities with (with the missing ingredient being that they may just not be what some (including yourself) consider ok to bring home). And from this you miss the point that love is not always about who comes off being the better deal in public (or the best REPRESENTAION (with her not necessarily being it) or what you think a wife is) but how they make you feel when all those whose approval you seek are gone) something being another consequence of doing things out of order with a sense of arrogance (with you feeling that you have a right to do what you do), vanity (from you being overly concerned with what other people think), and self righteousness (where you decide another's worth by judging them) being the motivating force behind this behavior so again don't start none (with you putting yourself in the position of incurring trouble) won't be none (with you avoiding another chokehold in your life). Ex. You trying to have your cake and eat it to by living a double life, with you still being intimately involved with the old lover (or someone new) all while maintaining what others see as a legitimate relationship with someone else.)*

f. The importance of self control. Now here again is another point previously discussed with the main advantage being you not so easily tempted when awkward situations arise. However this first starts with you either operating the way you should be initially or recommitting yourself to doing it by practicing the art of abstaining with you learning how to keep yourself. Some of the major benefits of doing this is the trust factor you gain when the person you are currently dating knows that you are not so easily moved when possible situations of compromise **arise** (*like you two getting hot and bothered while spending time alone together with her seeing that though you wanted to go there you chose not to*) **and** by her seeing this with it happening enough times to convince her that you do have a hand on things, she will not be so **threaten** (*or at least she shouldn't be; with her, if she is, being the instigator of her own problems because of her desiring you to do something you shouldn't be doing; something which when does happen causes you to look down on us for being a ball of contradictions when we call you out for calling us out*) **when** things outside of either of your control come into **play** (*like when you are away on trips etc; because she knows that you are able to turn it off*). **Remember** the more you operate off the "on the fly" premise the more irresponsible you look thereby causing us to feel insecure anytime an opportunity to stray is presented. Another advantage of learning the art of discipline, as it relates to point (a), is when things like distance do come into play especially when it's for long periods of **time** (*like in situations where you both live in two different cities or even with you serving time, cause yeah we've heard about what goes on in prison, (something all showing how anything goes when you reduce sex down to just an act with there no longer being boundaries)*) **by not** allowing loneliness to get the best of you, something when it does can bring about unwanted consequences like pregnancy, disease, dissention in the relationship or emotional entanglements with you having to face the music eventually because of it and possibly losing your relationship as well. Now another important point coming out of this is maintaining headship during times where your wife tries to use sex as a weapon from wanting to get her way (*something when your partner is able to achieve (with again her being able to manipulate you) could lead you to stray from you now needing to regain your manhood in someway*). And with her seeing that you aren't so quick to waiver, you have a greater chance of your desires being heeded or at least heard. In reference to this particular point (*with us not appreciating why we shouldn't be operating out of order*) is why this becomes a difficult task for most. Something I hope (*with what all I am saying*) **will** get you to say humm with you really looking at your behavior, learning to see things from a different perspective where a desire to do things correctly should hopefully occur. Other things to consider also here from this is you becoming more patient once family and/or work related issues start taking precedence over your love life with you being ok about it when it does. And from you not being able to get any kind of satisfaction at that particular moment, you'll hopefully begin to understand that like with anything else everything does have its appropriate time (*you know just like when you eat, sleep, etc.*) with you remembering that taking the "you can't always do what you want when you want to do it" stance will keep things in its proper perspective (*a mindset that would definitely get you through times of hindrance like when your partner is having a PMS moment where you know what's up (or what ain't gonna be up)*, **long** term health issues that could greatly impact the physical aspect of your relationship, or as a couple your wanting to practice natural birth control methods. Side note: Working together as a team could help alleviate some of these issues so again keep that in mind during trying times. And what I mean by this is if you are the primary breadwinner with you having a stay at home wife, she of course should be expected to hold up her end by her maintaining the household responsibilities, however as far as the kids are concerned since they are a joint venture you need to be doing whatever you can in order to lend a helping hand by spending the kind of time with them that would allow her to regroup from having to focus on both all day. Now in scenarios where you are operating off of two incomes you should have no problem rolling up your sleeves with you helping out by getting in where you fit in; and from doing so you create a situation where you should have time for each other. (*Side note for women here: Going back to the point about us withholding just to get our way (or us just not being all that interested), because sex was made for marriage and what Yah requires humans to do (by getting married first) when we do choose to satisfy our flesh, blowing your husband needs off is really not an option with us learning the art of good time management (if that is the problem or us getting over ourselves, realizing if he is still required to provide a home for* *us we have no other choice but to be handling our business in the bedroom). And since in most cases (during the dating stage) we were quick to give it up then it would be reasonable to expect that this is what your now husband thought he would be getting on a regular basis (something explaining why you shouldn't have used sex as the bait to hook a man, especially since you had no business doing it anyway). Besides if genuine affection between him and you truly does exist there should be a mutual desire for it with you (during trying times) now being even more motivated to restructure some of your priorities in order to make sure that neither of you are sexually deprived. Knowing that there is a difference between can't and won't (with can't garnering understanding and won't creating temptation) you again need to understand that with won't you are deliberately withholding something that he has a right to receive with you also understanding that when you play these kinds of games and he becomes weary, you are creating a state of discontentment where now he too may no longer be all that interested in fulfilling his obligations, etc. Something else from this is by playing your hand in this manner you are also saying to him that it wasn't about him that you got married for but more about what he either brings to the table that garnered acceptance of his offer (something done for the sake of being taken care of; or you now being able to start a family with the circumstances being once you got the kids he no longer is of importance anymore (outside of his financial support, with him being looked upon as just a sperm donor)); or you just wanting to have the presence of a man in your life. All of which can deeply hurt his feelings and why resentment comes into play. Something else important to remember here is that for men sex is a source of comfort with it also being looked upon as a form of affection. So fulfilling ALL your wifely duties by making sure that he is taken care of guarantees you certain rewards (like when things in the relationship go sour (with him moving on) where now you have the right to expect a return of investment (monetary payout) for your efforts. Because during the lean years you comforted him (with it giving him the ability to carry on) or during his years of growth (through your comforting, you were supporting him (with his focus being that much more clearer because of his desire to see it through from you being part of the picture)). And lastly something else relating to this point is why we should not be looking to be one of those who adds stress to his life by being a nag (or argumentative, something when we do can bring about abusive behavior), disinterested, or mean spiritedness with us operating off the thinking that since everybody else is already riding him hard why can't I, except for the fact that part of the reason he is taking so much off of everybody else is so he can be the man he needs to be for you and his family. With it also being if you are the one who is the provider (because of his lackings (from not having it together (from things falling apart or him not being able to execute his plans initially because of him chasing behind you or you just sidetracking him from you desiring a commitment where he was forced to give up on his dreams (something in either case being you never giving any thought to the kind of impact this might have later on as far as the kind of quality of life you'd have as a couple)) then what you got is what you get, just like if you knew he was not wise or truly dutifully with you marrying him anyway; something all saying that you can't just turn things off with you having no other choice but to just suck it up by making the best of the situation; something that one day might garner you the rewards you desire; because again if you had wanted better then you should've held out for something better, one that might have motivated you in a way where you would always be able to fulfill your wifely duties*)).

g. This point relates to (b) and (c) with us being able to differentiate between lust and love. Now of course we know that lust eventually fades once reality sets in however if you base your decisions to proceed on it and things like marriage and/or children again come out of this alliance, you will definitely be paying the piper with you either catching hell if she doesn't appreciate your sudden change of heart or getting a bad rep from not wanting to take responsibility for your **actions** (*do I dare say Eddie Murphy and Melanie Spice, where though he does pay child support, he was still looked upon as not being fully responsible because of his lack of involvement with the child. (Side note: Through a reconciliation recently orchestrated by his first wife, Nicole, the two have ironed out their differences and he is now actively part of the child's life, something showing how all parties involved can be affected by such actions since the former Mrs. Murphy felt their children were suffering from the stance he took, and why, in situations such as this, we need to put more thought into our decisions before making moves like this, especially when others look to us to be an example*)) **and** that again is one of the problems with lust because of its fleeting nature with it only being based on selfish **motivations** (*or lack of discernment with you not seeing things clearly*) something again once the person's needs have been met they lose interest and not just for the other person involved but from whatever resulted from **it** (*or maybe not if they do decide to take responsibility for their actions with a possible tug of war occurring because of it*), with it being totally unfair to the injured parties as well as possibly anyone coming after them because of foolishness that might be laid in their lap, with them now having to deal with this drama. Of course then there is you the perpetrator with you resenting that you still have to be bothered with this person at all; with you possibly taking your frustrations out on anybody who will let you if you choose not to own up to the part you played in this mess you created for yourself. Something you need to do because if you don't you will continue to carry this resentment to other relationships with you feeling that you were the one who got shortchanged from again operating off the concept that you could go for yours without consequence. Something leading to the next point.

h. Now from point (g) we get into "if you participated you can't escape it" meaning you can't point fingers when you're part of the situation (*or label me a ho without addressing your own behavior first*); something that seems to be a big problem for you, and again something that seems to make very little sense (*as far as I'm concerned*) with absolutely no merit being behind this reasoning. So the question here then is why do you feel that you are exempted from the crime of premarital (*or adulterous*) relations (*being with all these different women, leaving us left holding the bag*) even in times when you were the one who initiated it (*I guess having a penis has its privileges, huh; with you using it as an excuse to justify your actions*). Now I know most men will say that boys will be boys with them feeling that they have a right to partake of whatever is available to them, at least until things blow up in your face with you now suddenly having to deal with the consequences and that's when then it becomes our fault; whether it's taking advantage of your sudden vulnerability (*remember the penis thing where you start thinking with it*) with our womanly ways being the culprit in all of this or you following the path that was laid out for you where you are now able to blame society (*or upbringing*) by the way in which men as a whole are defined; something to a small extent does give you a pass for this discretion, however, after those first initial years of trial and error is when you are no longer excused (*because of what should have happened, which is you garnering wisdom from these experiences*) and this is exactly what this point is about. Continuing to blame ill beliefs (*or stupidity*) is whack (*or random*) and why when you do we as women become disillusioned with us seeing the nature of who you truly are, a coward (*or little boy*) in a man's (*or king's*) clothing. If you're big and bad enough to do it you should be able to handle whatever comes out of this action. Sex is not for little boys but for those who understand the importance of accountability (*as well as responsibility*); an action not only for the purpose of physical stimulation but something that creates life so taking it lightly is just not an option. Another problem with this relates to you blaming us for what is solely your decision to do with the only motivation being behind your desiring us in the first place is just you wanting to jack off. I mean what does it say about you as a person that you'd willingly involve yourself with those who you would never want to be seen (*or bothered*) with in otherwise respectable **circumstances** (*or in cases where there's really nothing to be ashamed of but them just having served their purpose*), **something** which when does happen could find you denying just to save face afterwards. Now if I'm not mistaken intimacy usually involves the act of sexual intercourse, something you are doing with women who you deem to be of lesser value than the one you have chosen (*or will choose*) to be committed to and you wonder why your partner treats you in the manner in which she does when trying to explain your way out of these kinds of **messes** (*something again that makes very little sense, cause for me if I'm going down I'm doing it in a big ole way with only the fly-est guy I can find (I mean anything else would be an insult to my man, right); with me only apologizing for getting caught (no just kidding)*) but again what all this shows is how thinking with the little head instead of the one Yah gave you to use for the purpose of discernment is detrimental to your well being and why the already above mentioned points directly applies to this one with you truly having a lack of respect for all **women** (*and yes this even includes the one you say you love from making a fool out of her, misleading her into believing that she's got it like that*), **Yah**'s word (*with you disregarding it*) **the other woman** (*from wanting to use* *her*), and lastly yourself (*for not aspiring to be the man we need you to be (with you not being someone we can trust or depend on; something that not only incurs this kind of outcome but also what could cause you to fall from your position of headship with us now feeling we have to manage you; something again leading you into an even more dysfunctional relationship where a vicious cycle of foolishness becomes never ending*)) **Excuses** like lack of self control will not get you out of unwanted pregnancies, emotional entanglements (*fatal attractions*), or STDS that could occur with your partner possibly suffering along with you in someway; something from which again goes back to showing your true lack of regard for others from having bad judgment (*or you just being selfish*). Also something else to remember here is if you're working off the principle that it is ok to sow your oats in this manner with you expecting your future partner to have not then get ready for possible disappointment. And how do you decide who will be the victim in this crime anyway or better yet what happens when all men feel this way (*oh yeah I forgot you do all feel this way*) with women in general being looked upon as fair game with again the philosophy being what is gold to one is silver to another; something putting us in the position of trying to live up to unrealistic expectations from innocence already lost. In this day and time, with most of society being less than virtuous, gives us very little credence to think that those we see as potential mates would not have a past and just like we have to live with yours you have no other choice but to live with ours with you working off the understanding that you don't have a right to judge. Now getting back to the soul tie issue with us again being eternally connected to those we've been intimately involved with, coming to terms with the fact that if they weren't someone you wanted this kind of alliance with, you can't, just because you decided to move on, erase these experiences, something again all saying why you need to stop working off the kind of thought processes that are leading you into believing that you can with you no longer allowing things that only require self control in the preventing of these kinds of circumstances to dictate your decisions instead of you just getting a hand on it (*through prayer, guidance, and a real desire to do the right thing*). Something again that could put you in a better light with those you care or will eventually care about. Question: How do you know the kind of person you are dealing with if you are seeking out sex yourself! And what I mean by this is with all that comes out of being intimate, with you desiring to avoid consequences of this nature, if you decide to hold back, when pursuing romantic ventures, by not going there and the person you are involved with pushes the issue of sex anyway (*with her disregarding your feelings about not doing so*) you would clearly be able to determine her agenda because someone coming correct would respect your feelings instead of ignoring them. However if you do pursue these kinds of endeavors with you desiring to quench your sexual thirst, her reason for going along with this could be numerous with uncertainty still existing as to what kind of person she is, something giving credence as to where having double standards can work against you because as long as you allow things that have the potential to blind side you it becomes easy to fall in another's trap.

i. Sex got you by the balls? Now the difference between point (c) and this one is what was mentioned previously being primarily rooted out of obligation where as here your decision for staying is based on your own desire to from your now lover turning you out (*you know like with you not being able to get enough of that funky stuff*). Of course the obvious danger in the latter is again not seeing clearly with you easily getting caught up. Remember tasting the water before you should can blind side you with you not being able to let go of something that may not have your best interest at heart. And being able to pull your lustful heartstrings to keep you in **line** (*or from you now being considered a fatal attraction* (*or sprung*) *yourself* (*something relating to this point in some ways and point* (*g*) *in a lot of ways*)) **is** how a person is able to bluff you into committing to them by backing you into a corner (*or you forcing issues by seizing control over them*) and again what I mean by this is if one of the women you are dating is aware that competition is in her mist, with them now wanting to run game (*from her desiring to be the one*) might resort to using the pullback **move** (*something where she sternly lets you know that she chooses not to just be a notch on your belt* (*something again of course that now intrigues you even more with you feeling this person must have scruples to play this hand*)); **something,** if she is successful in achieving the vantage point she desires from doing so, is what could lead you into believing that she is someone who is definitely into the chase, an outcome that could ultimately result in you unintentionally overlooking flaws that need to be addressed; something again all being because of you thinking that you are getting something special until you realize that you have absolutely nothing in common with this **person** (*or that they are just plain ole drama, with her not being in the least bit interested in making things work as she continues to ride the "it's my way or the high way" train*). **Now** again you may ask what does this example have to do with this particular point, well with most understanding the dynamics of how being **superficial** (*or judgmental with you looking at her as being the prize all while downgrading the other women in your life*) **can** play into things, it's easy to see the way in which one could fall into this kind of trap especially when too much focus is placed on **sex** (*or in this case the lack of, with the other party working off the hope that your desire for it will be that much more great*) **instead** of the overall values of a person you are interested in becoming romantically involved with; something in turn when women know this is how we are able to use this information as an aid in helping us get to the finish line quicker and why again when you put such great emphasis on this issue you can find yourself vulnerable to someone else's foolishness or your own if you're not able to differentiate between true virtue and self serving ambitions. Other issues coming out of this stems from your willingness to risk everything just to maintain an ill fated situation (*with you losing your self-respect, family, friends and position in the community because of it*). Having the proper perspective about intimacy (*with you not seeking sex out initially*) could help in adverting issues such as these (*from us developing unhealthy attachments or reaping what we sow because of how we treat others*) tremendously because there would be no consequence to deal with. Something else to keep in mind here is since most men desire a virtuous woman it's important that you yourself exhibit these same qualities in an authentic way; something unfortunately not always feasible due to how society defines men as a whole with us expecting you to come ready made that's why in most cultures better acquainting young men with sex through prostitution (*or known loose older women*) was an acceptable practice, something again considered by most to be a sort of right of passage into manhood with these same young men now being able to share this knowledge with their chosen mates from now being well qualified to please her. However once the sexual revolution came into play men don't have to look to paid sexcapades for expanding their horizons with them now being able to pick and choose who they please for this purpose; something resulting in degradation on a much broader scale with it driving a greater wedge between men and women. Whether it be a few or many once the seed of foolish was planted with men feeling that it is their Yah given right to pursue to the fullest the desires of their flesh was when the process of losing our souls began and the only way things will ever change is when society (*yes this includes women as well because of our own misguided concepts on how we define men*) learns to stop looking at sexual conquest as a part of **masculinity** (*a thought process that as it continues to poison our outlook, will cause greater mayhem (or foolishness) with things getting progressively worst, from men garnering a greater sense of entitlement because as our thirst for adventure increases, with us opening ourselves to different experiences, so does what now becomes available to explore*). **Side** note: For women who are reading this, growing up, a lot of us were led into believing that because this is a man's world, we, for the most part, have to accept a lot of their behavior especially as it relates to infidelity. And from this with men being able to justify their actions by claiming the ones they are committed to publicly versus those they continue to play with **secretly** (*or by how they interact with the other woman through the lack of financial benefit she receives (or in some instances with the man not doing certain things sexually with the jump off that he will do with his significant other and visa versa with him having different expectations for the main woman with the side piece picking up where she left off)*), **they** attempt to not only alleviate some of the guilt behind it for themselves but also pacify us as well; something that initially may work for a while with us operating off the premise that as long as I'm getting mine who cares. However once we come to the conclusion that all we are doing is nothing more than man **sharing** (*with us now again having to deal with the seedy mess of his consequences (from again unwanted pregnancies, STDS, emotional entanglements where the jump* *off is no longer satisfied in just being one (or how she is being treated because of being one))* **where** now suddenly the presence of these liaisons are thrusted to forefront for all the world to see (*do I dare say Jesse James or Tiger Woods*), we become weary with us realizing that no amount of pacifying will be able to change the fact that we may never achieve the goal of being all the woman he needs and that we have been wasting a lot of time thinking that we could. And that's what we are left with, something not suppose to be but unfortunately what we choose to make it be, when we settle with it being based on our desire to be attached and/or taken care of. Which in some ways is part of the problem with men knowing how to play the game (*just like in the same way we do when we use sex to hook them*); something all explaining why this kind of **foolishness** (*with us now needing to protect our vested interest by tripping all the time; something that could further push him into the arms of another*) **has** and will continue with the only way things changing is when all women desire better (*remember a person will only be able to do to you what you allow them to do*), with us not being so quick to accept an offer just because someone offered; an outcome that may force men to see things differently. Also something else to consider here (*outside of you eventually feeling shortchanged from putting up with your man antics*) is though you may be reaping the benefits as the main woman, understanding that by not caring about how the way in which he treats others is like not being concerned about how he may eventually treat you because you are encouraging him to continue behavior that should be discouraged and why when it comes back around to you the hurt is even that much more greater. Understanding that the sexual revolution has worked more against women than men, with them no longer being limited to looking to their significant other as a source for physical satisfaction, something making the problem child of temptation not only his cross to bear but ours as well; with instead of indiscretions being just based on repairable issues (*such as lack of communication, distance, etc.*) they are now based on well established behavior that we as women **encouraged** (*like with us wanting him to make us drop it like it's hot initially; experience he had to garner from somewhere else otherwise he would be labeled as being a lame from his inability to*). **And** again from us using sex for one purpose and him benefiting from it is why being casual has bitten us in the butt with him riding the tide for as long as he can and us left holding the bag, think about it!

j. Getting yours before you should, the advantage of it just being between you and your chosen mate is not having to share this experience with others. Bringing this to a close, this next to last point deals with the consequence of spreading oneself too thin from cheating ourselves out of what makes intimacy so special. When you look at how we deal with our mate's past you have to wonder why people still continue working off the thought processes that casual sex (*or physical relationships outside of our marital one*) is ok. Throughout this section, I have touched on this issue from time to time so again forgive me for being repetitious with me hopefully expounding in such a way that you gain further insight. Now with most men being aware that women outnumber them by at least 4 to 1 it is understandable why you would feel justified in believing that with so many available to love why not go for it; except again until you decide to settle down where now you find yourself in the position of trying to leave the past behind. Something that should make you say **hummm** (*you know like with you thinking that if you hadn't ran through women like water you would have came into your marriage on a clean slate, where whatever happens in your bedroom being sacred, something just being between you as a couple with you learning from each other as opposed to basing things on experience learned from others that neither your partner nor you can really cherish without hurting the other's feelings*). **Now** are you beginning to see the kind of problems this can cause. And because of this, how we relate to those outside of the relationship is also greatly affected where we now have to diminish their importance in our **lives** (*something mention earlier I know, a situation most feel ok about it until the shoe is on the other foot where those you were there for have now dismissed your efforts because of their significant other with you feeling like why did I even care in the first place, again it is important to remember that life is a journey and from this there are people who were part of our lives for a reason, with the problem being then is how we looked at intimacy with us giving too much of ourselves when it wasn't merited*) **as** well as us being left with regret from realizing that we can't take those no longer precious moments **back** (*or make somebody something they can't be, like your first with the consolation in this being for them that they are the one you chose to spend the rest of your life with* (*or another way of looking at it is though your old love may have won the battle, it's your wife who's won the war so unless she is slipping there ain't too much reason for her* (*or you for that matter*) *to be tripping*)), **with** us finally getting it that physical intimacy is really meant to be shared between two people who are truly committed to each other; something where it doesn't matter how wonderful those past relationships were, with us now secretly wishing that they had never happened. You know I hear so many people talk about, after finding that special person, how much they would love to turn back the hands of time and do it right the way; with it not being just because of the residue left behind from these former liaisons, but them really desiring to have only shared this gift with their mates, with them seeing the value in doing things this way. Even when attempts to set a good example for their kids come into play (*because they themselves didn't follow the righteous path*) they now find it difficult to talk to their children about intimacy without feeling apologetic. Something they should be able to get past with them understanding that experience can sometimes be the best teacher with us becoming a better person because of it. The only problem here is when we do learn from our mistakes does it really benefit others if they think because we got through the storm that maybe they too could still do the same by following in our footsteps. Something unfortunately that becomes another burden to bear with us working off the hope that they don't take our failings lightly with them again also understanding that since sex is not the bases (*at least for most sensible people with the ones who do regretting it*) in which why we choose who we choose as a life partner then it makes very little sense to put such great emphasis on it up front. And what I mean by this is from all the sexual encounters that we've had, how many of those involved were considered marriage material (*probably only a few*) with again the point being that no matter how great the sex was (*between whoever did or didn't make the cut*) there was probably other qualities that took precedence. Also from this is when all factors (*consideration, patience, and good communication*), along with Yah's presence, are right it becomes easy to teach the other person ones likes and dislikes, with it saying that you don't have to be an expert initially with both learning each other in a way that as you grow in the love making process you also grow in experience with you now becoming uniquely one together, the way it is truly suppose to be. One of the things we tend to forget is that sex is part of the covenant of marriage where our bodies are now that of our mates so when you are out there doing your thing you're actually giving away pieces of what belongs to the one you will eventually pledge your love, life, and devotion to; something explaining why adultery is such a big deal with the consequence being severe when we choose to take our vows for granted; something that makes perfectly good sense because of the entailed sacrifice each party is required to **make.** (*Side note: With men not usually being taught to look at their bodies as a precious vessel, in the same way we are, they again tend to not put a lot of thought into why they should be more discerning when it comes to intimacy, with it being, if they did, them not being so irresponsible, from knowing that they too should be desiring something other than random situations.*) **Another** point that becomes important for our offsprings to understand is that in most cases our inability to wait stems from selfish motivation where **arrogance** (*from feeling entitlement* (*something relating to men with them feeling that whatever they desire is theirs to have until the drama they incur from it becomes not worth it or they get a conscience from again knowing that they got off at somebody else's expense*) **insecurity** (*with the person desiring to prove themselves* (*again a man's problem*) *or fear of lost* (*something that usually relates to women with us learning the hard way that no matter how much we drop it like it's hot you as well as those who follow you still probably won't commit*)), **manipulation** (*this again relates to women, where because of us being aware of your thirst for sex we use your weakness to our advantage with us now being to get our way by running game*), **or** just plain old fear where because of one being hurt (*or afraid of being hurt*) we choose to give only so much of ourselves with us having full intentions of backing out of it when we feel justified in doing so; and what makes this reasoning worst than the other three is from knowing better where not treating people the way we want to be treated being behind it; where again the main objective here is achieving our goals, that's why so much drama is usually attached to it because instead of us choosing the kind of situation where we shouldn't be looking to walk away from (*like marriage*) we choose what is temporary (*dating or courtship*) with it being something we can walk away from. And these are some of the lessons we hope will deter our children in a way that they make better choices. (*Side Note: In regards to the dating customs of today and the problems it creates from boundaries being blurred. With people treating the boyfriend/girlfriend thing in the same manner they treat marriage, courtship takes on a more than usual obligating tone, with couples now actually behaving as if they were; something occurring when things like sex, time invested (where greater consideration of the other is given) and financial benefits, truly do become part of the picture. With the problem being once marriage comes into play, things (namely sex) that were once considered optional are still looked upon that way even though they aren't anymore (1 Corinthians 7:3-5), leaving men having to still negotiate for it just to get it; from the mindset of their mate never changing. It's important to remember that dating and marriage are two different entities with one created for the purpose of growing in knowledge of a person (something that MAY OR MAY NOT lead to marriage) with the other being the institution one or both are striving to get to. And with that being said, when boundaries are not established discontentment can set in once things become permanent from the feeling on what's changed now that they are. Something, if you don't believe me, just check out the statistics of those choosing to live together before holy matrimony and the number of divorces following afterwards.*)

k. Another thing to consider here, is the woman's stance, "it's my body not yours". With me saying, why put yourself in the position of being at the mercy of someone else's whim where now you have to deal with whatever direction they choose to take (*meaning, if they choose to have a baby, child support and added responsibilities regardless if you moved on or not, or abortion, heartbreak*) when proper behavior (*abstaining*) could have avoided situations like this, because after all it is your sperm right, with you also having some say on how it is going to be utilize. Remember not all men are irresponsible, with them being ok about doing right thing by their child. But as we all know, a man's feelings is no longer considered when outcomes such as these occur. That's why waiting until you are in a sanctioned relationship (*marriage*) where if something like this did happened, you BOTH should at least be in the CORRECT mindset that would allow you to better handle the concept of pregnancy from you both knowing that this is something that naturally comes with the territory.

The most important point coming out of this discussion is that doing things out of order brings about great consequence. Since the beginning of time there has been a certain way in which how relationships formulate with Yah putting a burning fire of desire in men's souls and women being created to receive it; something causing us to become easily attached when pursued with you exploiting what you see as being weakness when the need **arises** (*a situation occurring once sin entered into the picture with it creating a division between not only* *man and Yah but also between man and woman as well; something also resulting in man now working off his own foolish council (or limited understanding) with him rewriting his life's story as he see fits. That's why, when romantic endeavors fail, the burden as to how it did falls on your shoulders. I mean because after all you were the one given headship; something where when your motives are questionable or based on naïve concepts (with you not assessing things correctly) we now become the victim of these pursuits instead of a joint benefactor (remember you would be getting yours here). Something also explaining why when it does come to ventures such as this your decision to proceed should* **MOSTLY (but not exclusively)** *be based on good common sense and not on frivolous things where eventually their importance will no longer matter. (An additional side note to this is even with that being said because women have also been equipped with discernment as well makes us just as accountable for our actions so though you pursued us again we didn't have to accept once things became apparently clear that the reasoning behind your desire to couple up wasn't right)).* **And** from this is where our problems began because we have chosen to take things into our own hands with us now no longer having access to Yah's true vision for our lives as we now go through a series of hit or misses scenarios before eventually achieving some kind of success; something where even if there are casualties we still feel exonerated because in our eyes all that mattered was that we accomplished the goal of sealing the deal. Basing things on lustful desires leads to disastrous results and with us not fully understanding why we should not be allowing these vices to take precedence over our better judgment hinders us further. Now with all that has been said about premarital sex, understanding that a lot of trial and error in the dating process (*where we play the wait see and game*) could have been avoided if we had chosen to wait on Yah with him bringing someone into our lives who he knows will be able to walk through this journey of life together with; something only happening after all that needs to happen as far as working out the **kinks** (*you know like emotional dysfunctions or professional challenges; something when these things are out of sync can create a means to an end mentality where now we start using people with things continuing this way until we are in a better place* (*a circumstance where karma will probably be playing a major role in changing our direction*)) **in** our life goes that's why we need to trust in his timing instead jumping ahead before we are **ready** (*something when we do could bring about disillusionment for all parties involved with it now causing those considered victims of this foolishness to in turn return the favor by hurting others*) **and** in some cases even creating an outcome that cannot be **rectified**. (*Side note: One sure fire way of knowing if a situation is something to heed to is if you find it hard to unleash your self serving interest on someone else because deep down you know that you truly do care about this person; with again the situation being that if it takes very little effort to show lack of regard for a person like this, it probably wasn't meant to be anyway however even with that it still becomes important in how the way you leave a person with them knowing that you are not a dog; something that will allow them to move on in a more positive way and you not left with the guilt that you were*). **With** it all saying that until the slate is clean with us operating under the correct mindset we need not be doing anything outside of Yah's directive. Something relating to some of the problems with casual dating, especially when sexual desires are looking to be quench; and again why dating with the intention to marry is more valid than dating for temporary **purposes** (*where you are now wasting the other person's time (a point going back to why you are held more accountable*); *with it being that even though you desire some kind of companionship, deception may now becomes part of the pursuit*) **with** the former allowing us to get to the finish line of love in a more appropriate manner (*without the drama of foolishness to deal with unless you rely too much on your own judgment with you jumping into something that is truly wrong for you*). So in closing all that has been suggested or implied (*as it relates to dating with friendship being incorporated into it*) is based on what may work if you choose to go it alone without bringing Yah into it. However if you take the best route you can take (*something applying to everybody which is Yah's loving guidance, with it bringing you back to the relationship we were all destined to have originally.*) you will be guaranteed to have a more certain and fulfilling **union**. (*Side note: Because Yah sometimes places us in certain situations in order to get us from point a to b he may use friendship as his way of directing you to the person you are suppose to be with; with the difference being in this scenario versus you becoming friends first with you then deciding to date the person later (after seeing that there could be something worth pursuing) is here you would not be proceeding unless Yah instructed you to where with the latter situation your moving forward would most likely be based on the comfort zone you have with this person, with it still not necessarily working out; something with the advantage being that at least you already know that you and the other person were compatible instead of finding out once things went any further that you weren't, if things had started out strictly on a romantic basis first.*) **And** that's it, my take on why I say the problem with men is sex. Where with you putting too much emphasis on it has corrupted your spirit with it causing you to not only possibly be distracted (*with your priorities being wrong, something that could hinder you from finding or appreciating your mate, as well as your purpose*) but to also have a perverted concept about how things in your relationships should play out. It is important to remember that though Yah made us sexual beings there was a reason why he wanted this aspect of romance harnessed in the compounds of marriage with him being fully aware of what would happen if our desire to quench it went outside of it with the question now being do you?

FOOTNOTE: A good reference point from the bible is the story of David, with you seeing how he allowed his desires to get the best of him destroyed his family and reputation as well as the story of Sampson.

THE POWER OF LOVE AND SELF ACCEPTANCE

Chapter Five

Black Men Issues Continued

Why is being a black man

such an issue for you

Understanding Why You Can't Continue Keeping the Good Man Inside Of You Down

Well just like how I ended the women's section of this book with black issues being discussed, I wanted to do the same here with me also addressing some of the problems that seem to plague us as a people in general, and black men in particular. Issues I feel if not addressed will eventually create the kind of divide between us as a race that may eventually become irreparable. Understanding our history is important because as the saying goes "If don't know where you come from you . . .". Something we all have heard throughout our formative years with us for the most part ignoring the importance of what our elders have been trying to convey as to why we should care. Because with our self esteem seemingly attached to how others see us (*with what we have contributed to this country being largely ignored*) it definitely becomes imperative that we know what we were and still are capable of accomplishing. With the reason being when we do, we realize no one outside of our race can define us by the vision they have mapped out for us (*or their take on who they think we are*); with us now being able to forge ahead pursuing our purpose filled destiny. And by allowing others to reshape our futures through oppression we only see what they see with us eternalizing self loathing, giving credence to another well known saying that goes "if you don't love yourself you can't love anybody else". Now again with us having such contempt for each other with us chasing behind our **oppressors** (*something that in itself is asinine, I mean why would anybody with any kind of sense want to emulate those who want to keep them down; with them constantly diminishing our self worth,* *and in a lot of ways even contradicting themselves; with this also being against Yah's will as well)*

Proverbs 3:31:32

Do not envy the oppressor, and choose none of his ways, For the perverse person is an abomination to the Lord.

Getting into a few of these just mentioned points here is if one has no value then why would another desire their **presence** (*cause personally I would not have went through all the trouble of bringing over another group of people without making sure there would be some permanent benefit (oh yeah I forgot, they needed labor, with them not having any intention of it being temporary that's why they're still mad about it huh!) except now we are considered to be lazy and shiftless something that I would say has validity if the playing field was leveled with us being given the same rights as they have (something we know is not true) with us being put in the position of having to make due with whatever opportunities that have been made available to us; something even applying to those who slipped through the cracks by achieving some kind of success with them constantly being reminded on how they are walking on thin ice and what would happen if they ever choose to get out of line*). Another thing to think about here is if we truly are less than them why then would anybody feel threatened by us coming into our own and on our **terms** (*and what I mean by this is when self pride comes into play with us accepting ourselves others begin to feel annoyed or offended by this; something again that can have one scratching ones head because why would anybody be bothered by how another feels* *about themselves unless that is the only way the existence of superiority can stay rooted with us constantly being plague by what others see as inadequacies (or because when the other group begins to take pride in who they are the oppressor loses control over them; something I feel should motivate us to strive even more instead of succumbing to another's foolishness (or even worst because we are so much more less in their eyes that they feel why would any race of people want to be associated with what others consider to be nothing of importance as far as our history and culture goes or look beyond what mainstream has already deemed valid). With it also being important to understand that when you reinvent yourself instead of appreciating what Yah has already made you to be you are **actually spitting in his face** (remember we are here because of another's lackings with them not being able to tend to their own labor issues, so if they didn't like the package or what it consisted of then they should have left us be and just picked their own cotton; and from their continued blatant lack of regard for us is why we're still suffering as well as it now also being their own people with the powers to be treating us all like slaves in someway from them desiring to get something for nothing; a mindset which comes out of the thinking that it is ok to mistreat others, where again now because of greed no one is safe. Something if you don't believe me then ask yourself why are companies sending jobs overseas where they know they are able to get cheap labor with them also looking to no longer pay those here a decent salary with benefits; with the impact from their unreasonable demands being such that a lot of what we cherish the most (like time, family life, and our general well being) is now on the verge of collapse. Side note here: For those of the Caucasian persuasion who think slavery was such a good thing, remember free labor reduces a paid workforce thereby leaving a lot of those such as yourself without employment, something being one of the* reasons why the institution was abolished in the first place). And by putting someone else's opinion above the one we should be concerned about (I mean after all the reason for Yah allowing us to be part of what is called the human race in the first place stems from him desiring us to be here, with him having his own plans in mind for us; something all saying that when others attempt to undo (or redirect) his vision they are disrupting the natural order of things with the aimed target being completely turned around with them being lost and that is exactly what we are now a lost people without identity or home with us in so many ways being at the mercy of others; and from this we have as well turned on each other because of a desire to get ahead anyway we can with us seeking the approval of those who have neither a heaven or hell to offer anybody). Thirdly being concerned about those who act like they have no use for us on one hand with them being consumed with putting us in our place; with them again not allowing us to find our own way in order to change this condition all while having to listen to them constantly complain about us not pulling our weight on the other (with us as black people needing to ask our white counterparts the question which way do they really want it, because if you don't want us here then send us back, otherwise . . . . (something from what I understand was at one time planned, but never actually fully acted upon (meaning Liberia and Panama with us actually having the skills sets to see it through from our then ability to do so) due to opposition on both sides (which still doesn't exactly let you off the hook since the power to do so was always in your hands)) or if you do want us to stay with us continuing to be under the chokehold of oppression then also be ok about picking up the slack, otherwise . . . . or if you don't like who we are or what we look like then take it up with Yah, otherwise . . . .)). So again how can we be too concern about those who really don't know what they want outside of maintaining

the status quo of exalting themselves over others. Side note: One of my
pet peeves with white folks has to do with how they seem to be so
concerned about us taking over as far as us dating their women, sports,
industries, communities, etc. even though they are the ones either
constantly throwing up in our faces, images that tell us what we are
suppose to strive for (something causing us to desire it), separating us
from each other (where we now feel we have to fraternize or patronize
with those outside of our race, you know like with them limiting the
access of black men and women on college campuses (example football
and basketball players being recruited to primarily white universities
where availability to the other is almost non existence) or places of
employment where we have no other choice but to pursue them) or
hindering our progress (with us now again having no other choice but
to seek out what we see as being better opportunities, like schools,
housing, businesses; something that if we were able to also have in our
own communities with us benefiting from the same financial support,
redevelopment incentives or lending practices, we might stay put
instead of invading your territory), and because of this you force our
hand so again if you don't like what you created by instigating this
mess then stop boxing us in). **Now** as far as how we view
ourselves with us coveting another's qualities we have thrown
ourselves under the bus because of our own lack of regard for
our fellow brothers and sisters; remember we all bring
something to the table of life with these attributes
complimenting as well as enlightening others so discarding
them with us working off the hope that allowing someone
else's methods to take precedent instead of seeing value in our
own hinders our progress with us utilizing limiting concepts
(*or one way of doing things, something that sounds like the making of*
robots) and without learning how to integrate or interject any

possible contributions we might have into the mix, we now deny ourselves (*from some of us deciding not to rock the boat*) with it causing dissension within our group something again also explaining why there is such a great divide with some of us taking the position that others in our group who choose to go mainstream are betraying our **race.** (*Side note: There is nothing wrong with speaking correctly or having progressive desires from wanting a better life (except for the condescending attitude that goes along with it where you start looking down on others as though they were ignorant (a situation never addressed by those who choose to better themselves where now you become the target for being attacked, remember most of us are fully aware of who's really behind some of our ills with racism playing a very important part in this so when you take on these same attitudes those who look like you now see you as being the enemy with them coming after you because you are more accessible than those you choose to emulate)* **without** *considering that nobody is better than anybody else with them also harboring flaws and because of this you become the object of ridicule from discrediting yourself (something again once you realize this you should no longer be worshiping those you see as having a greater advantage with you now appreciating where from whence you came); that's why it doesn't make sense to take on attributes of somebody else because eventually you will be knock down as well. Something else to remember is we are suppose to be a blessing to each other so when you take on the "I'm above it all" attitude with you turning your back on your community it could come back to haunt you with you setting yourself up for the favor being returned when you one day need somebody; with it coming across to others who you are trying to impress that it was ok to treat us in the manner in which they have been doing because even you don't think enough of yourself to support that from which you came (or desire to* *reach back to help) with it meaning that when they get tired of you they will revert back to treating you much in the same way they treated those left behind so again think about it. Now for those who punish others for wanting to move forward it's important to understand that we're all suppose to aim for the best and not purposely continue to embrace that of an oppressive state, with it saying to those who are partially responsible for our demise this is where we want to be therefore again justifying their actions; something I know is a result of not loving oneself with us believing that we are not worthy of anything beyond what we are use to seeing. But we have to get past this because Yah does want us to be more than our circumstances with him creating us to make a difference in the world as we bring something to it in a positive way so to stay stuck in a negative mindset is displeasing to him. It becomes imperative that we worked together to support each other with it being the only way our conditions will change. Out of all the ethnic groups that exist we are the only ones who don't hence explaining why we are still in an oppressive state. Also Yah will never bless you with anything better if you don't know how to work with what you have already (something who knows may bring about greater blessings with those who thought they were handicapping us being astonished by our ingenuity because of us taking something that was thought to be nothing of value with them only seeing it that way through their eyes and us realizing its potential). One thing about black folks is that we are survivors with us knowing how to make a way out of no way; something others will eventually desire (I mean look at hip hop where how we took music sampling along with words and turned it into a multi-million dollar business, soul food making it a universally comfort cuisine, or blues, jazz etc. with it now being considered one of America's greatest home grown art forms and the list goes on, on the many ways they've* attempted to hinder us with them throwing us the scraps and us in turn making it great. Even the dress attire of **prisoners** (something I know a lot of us hate, but hey these guys made it work, with a question being directed to those who don't approve, what young black designer have you invested in to go up against these clothing lines, something that would give us an alternative (Yes I'm talking to you Ms. Winfrey, Mr. Cosby or to all these other so called professional people who if they saw this as an opportunity to seize (with it possibly bringing about job creation) could put their names on the map), I mean if you are not going to put your money where your mouth is then . . . . because that's the problem now, we complain about it but if they didn't exist what would we be left with except supporting those who really don't respect (or in some cases even want) our money. Something else relating to this is for all you filmmakers out there with it being that maybe if you invested in business ventures that brought about the kind of profits where you could financially back your own projects (with it also bringing about opportunities to future filmmakers and/or playwrights, etc.) you would no longer have to be at the mercy of Hollywood anymore; with it being even more so if you pulled all your resources together to make it happen.) **is** now again a multi-million dollar business (pants on the ground, pants on the ground) and that's how you know there is a divine presence watching over us somewhere because when one group attempts to stop another Yah uses their foolishness to bless the group they attempted to hold back (the only problem here is us usually messing things up by exploiting it (or giving it away from easily discarding it) which is why it turns into our curse) so stop worrying about what you don't have and make what you do have work for you)). **Another** issue we need to deal with is our internal racial conflicts. Again it starts with us allowing others to define us, remember white people came over to Africa bringing us back to their many lands so in my opinion they need to get over whatever issues they have concerning what was already preordained by Yah, especially since we were in our land, minding our own business, a place where we were loved and cherished for our physical attributes something all saying that we have nothing to be ashamed of! Now as far as the fair skin/dark skin issues goes, if we would stop placing those who WE consider favored on a pedestal then they might stop feeling like they are so much better, besides a lot of those who carry these attributes are products of our oppressors so naturally they would probably exhibit some of these same attitudes because it is part of who they are. And being realistic anything that is part of the oppressor is going to be treated less harshly than those who are not hence explaining house and field slaves. Now what needs to change is the oppressor's attitude with them understanding that they are no better than anybody else an issue unfortunately we really can't force those who feel this way to see with it being left up to us to show them that beauty is not limited to one group's definition of it with us boldly celebrating who we are and from that they may eventually come to realize that we do deserve to be treated with higher regard. Because we are in coveted (*or stolen*) land and not **ours** (*something again that beckons the question as to why we would want to follow those who may eventually reap what they sow with us going down the ship with them if they continue to choose not to own up to it.*) **it** becomes difficult to get others to get past their own foolishness with us really needing to get past ours by no longer succumbing to the divide and conquer strategy with us again no longer allowing past wounds to get the best of **us** (*something* *where there still could be a few casualties with the ones who desire to continue holding on to negatives ideas going on their merry little way all while those of us who want to bridge the gap between the ones who are considered favored and those who aren't again no longer seeing color as an advantage anymore with NONE of us being ashamed of our physical attributes*). **Coming** from a multi hue family myself I appreciate and love the different variations of what represents African, Indian and possibly European descent. Besides of all the things I have come to realize is that color does not necessarily relate to origin with some of our darker hue people actually being descendents of Europe and not of Africa just like in turn our lighter hue folks descendents really coming straight off the boat; with the make up of who we are being based on the choices of our ancestors throughout the **years** (*meaning if someone from Europe produced a child with someone of African descent and that child continued mating with those of the latter their offsprings would have had a greater African lineage rather than European even though the top of the family tree started out that way and visa versa; something else to keep in mind is how genetics also plays an important part on our physical being where out of the blue an unexpected gene decides to make its presence known with it changing the dynamics of that person. Example: A black child being born with reddish brown hair with them not sharing that feature with either of their parents however upon further investigation you find out that one of the parents great-great-great grandmothers was of Irish descent with her having flaming red hair*). **That's** why making this a problem is again stupid because truth be told we really don't know what we are, even white folks might be surprise to find out who truly is the captain of this ship called a family (*sounds like the plot for a movie in the making, huh*)! Now one of the most

271

important points coming out of this, outside of loving yourself, is that it is a damn shame for us to still be harping on this issue especially when we're the main ones responsible for it from not being content with who we are as well as being the ones who keep bringing it up. Something that makes me wonder if some of our ancestors didn't deliberately **mix** (*instead of it being based on the violation of rape; something I know seems unspeakable but we have to keep in mind that even back then some of our ancestors were easily able to dime each other out when those choosing not to be slaves anymore wanted to escape with the motivation being the same, getting out of the fields, so it is quite possible that they very well could have chosen to take a route like this as well.*) **with** the reason behind all this hostility stemming from unfulfilled expectations. And what I mean by this is when we laid with our oppressors and a child came out of it, they now being the favored one most likely would have faired far better than that from which they came from. And because of this in order for them to survive they would have naturally wanted to disassociate themselves from those who they saw as being at a disadvantage because they didn't want to be in the same position. However that from which they came (*who is responsible for them being here (or planned it out this way)*) would have desired a return of investment by also receiving favor; something at that time could have jeopardized all what the favored one saw as benefits, with the penalty involved for doing such causing them not to do so hence leaving those from which they came with feelings of betrayal with it also resulting in creating this great divide. Now on the other hand if the favored person was a product of something negative (*like rape*) and they know this they probably would have turned away from the oppressor with them desiring not to have accepted whatever was being offered because of how things came about; also in cases such as this because the favored one knows firsthand what the oppressor is about (*because of the nature of their relationship with this person*) they realize all the hoopla is for not with them instead looking at what the oppressor considers to be less than having more value. Whereas when it is consensual that from which the favored one came from would've encourage their offspring to take advantage of what was seen as a blessed opportunity with them doing just that something which could possibly mean leaving that from which they came from out in the **cold** (*or karma from fraternizing with the oppressor and that's why we need to love all of who we are because when we don't we create situations like this with us compromising ourselves just to obtain a better life*). **Something** else relating to this example is when those who have successfully gotten out of the environment from which they came with them turning their backs on those who helped get them where they are (*like parents, grandparents, etc. who didn't want their loved ones exposed to other ignorant Negroes*). And with them now not seeing value in those who look like them (*remember this idea was embedded in their psyche growing up*) is what is bound to happen because they see no advantage in consorting with those from which they came including those who helped them get where they are, something again showing how prejudice from within can bite you in the butt because how you see yourself is how others will see you as well as with it feeding into the philosophy of those who want to follow these ill beliefs; with them moving further and further away from those who look like them because of **it** (*something for* *parents to think about when it comes to their children dating choices under circumstances like this with you discrediting yourself from expressing your displeasure over who they bring home with you knowing that they can't use your comb. Because after all if this is all that's available to date what other options do they have; something all again saying why as parents you can't continue to operate off the thought processes that you are the only BLACK parents on this earth who want a better life for their children with you understanding that there are others who feel as you do with it being left up to you (since you're the one who put your kids in this predicament) to seek those having the same like minds out instead limiting your social circle to just what you deem acceptable like, white folks). Another issue coming out of this is those of the darker hue only dating those of the lighter ones exclusively with them not understanding how they look and why when they get mistreated the reason behind it. Because like I said earlier in the text if a person knows that you only want them for superficial reasons they are going to go for theirs which means they are going to take advantage of the situation with you being left running on empty with the same being for the favored person who decides to date a person under the thinking that they now have the upper hand because of their desired attributes; something when the other person becomes aware of it they too will go for theirs with them pulling the rug out from under the favored person).* **Now** getting to the heart of the matter as to why black men continue to let race dictate their lives in such a way. With all that has just been said about not working with what we have all while letting others to define you *(those who them themselves have deficiencies (with them just having a good propaganda machine) and not appreciating who we are)* I hope you begin to see the importance of why you need to get past this. One of the problems with living in a racist society, is, as a black man, you being unable to map out your destiny in the same way as everybody else (*except however though through sexual conquest; something where you now have become very proficient in; with of course you feeling you can, in the context of a personal relationship, dominate us because that is the only place where you feel you can be all of what you think you are suppose to be; until now where we have suddenly gotten balls* (*a circumstance leaving you with nothing to work with. Side note: When you think of one of the greatest fears of the white man being your sexual prowess; something without them considering that they've turned into a self-fulfilled prophecy because of the limitations they've imposed on you; and being because of this you have to wonder why they still continue to box you in this way. Because again we know how to make the best of a situation with you finding a way to make this work for you. However though, like anything else that carries little weight its importance has diminish with you no longer being able to rely on it anymore because as sisters we are moving forward with you quickly losing ground. So now this is your dilemma, with the question being what is your plan of action, on how to overcome being the target of someone else's ills I mean outside of leaving with you going back to the mother land* (*a place where you already feel disconnected from*) *or do you venture out with you finding other uncharted lands but where because for the most part anything of value has already been claimed* (*outside of the purchase of private islands that could be brought up to livable environments, if the powers to be would allow it (or by force if we collectively sue on the bases of conditions we now are negatively existing under) and those who have the resources choose to make that kind of investment giving those who want to leave other options, Kanye and the likes, holla if you hear me; and where working with Africa and the Africa diaspora could possible bridge many gaps with us all working together*); *with the only thing being left is us looking to our own communities where we could work together for the good to create something great and on our terms (because again if you can get together to do destructive things why not for something positive from which you can grow into the kind of men Yah wants you to be with it causing others to take notice with them realizing that you do bring something to the table. Side note: Here when others on the outside see that we take pride in ourselves and our community it creates a desire to be attach to it as well. Keep in mind that nobody wants to be bothered with what is seen as being negative; something explaining why integration doesn't work when it's one sided, with you also understanding that others have to see value in what we have in order to commune with us otherwise they will continue running away and with our constant complaining about what we don't have instead of showing what we can do with it is what's keeping us down. Of course what a lot of you try to do is bring your support system (us, kids, friends) down with you attempting to discourage us from moving forward something that is slowly killing our race, with the mind set of our youth leaning toward self-destruction; something you will have to answer to (remember you are suppose to be the leaders in our community so we need you to be an example and not only just for the sake of our kids but for us as well with you as our warriors setting the tone; something, since we do desire your presence in our lives, may cause us to hold back from pursuing our goals just to maintain a relationship. Because we are designated to be a helpmeet we need someone to help; like in the same way a vice president needs a president with it being that we only take over when we have to otherwise what is the point in having you around at all with us instead of doing it ourselves or running you (with us leading you by the nose) from you being a man/child. (Side note: Being one of the many women who may never get married I am fully aware that Yah has equipped those of the same with the ability to not only stand on our own two feet but to also head boardrooms as well so to say we need you for any other reason than friendship wouldn't exactly make a whole lot of sense, however, in times where the natural order of things needs to be respected (like in the context of marriage) you should be taking charge in CERTAIN AREAS thus explaining why we do need you to be all what you are suppose to be; something involving you having a solid foundation to go on.) Again allowing others to define you instead of the one who wanted you here (Yah) is what is leading us to continue mapping out a foolish destiny something that could eventually bring us back to slavery if things continue and that's what the prison system is legalize slavery with you now doing work for little or nothing with our oppressors continuing practices (like trumped up charges, lack of opportunities, racial profiling, etc.) that keeps this a never ending vicious cycle and being why I keep saying we have to turn our disadvantages into advantages otherwise we will never get out of this mess (and you getting your spiritual life together is key in this happening because as you develop a personal relationship with Yah, with him showing you his vision and giving you the tools to help you get there (something allowing you to get your hustle on in a more positive way)* **you will be able to get around what others deny us of. Spending time dwelling on what we don't have is getting us no where** *(and why we hold anybody who looks like us down because of the mentality of "If I can't have it then neither can they" something building a permanent wall of mistrust between each other))*. **Now** before wrapping this up, I want to get into a few other points not mentioned as well some that have with us delving a little more deeper:

a. The price for chasing behind another's ideal of success; something a little different than from allowing others to define you (*with someone telling you who you are suppose to be*) with it being here that you find yourself going along with what others deem valid (*like achieving what others see as being the American dream where values, self image, ideology, etc. are thrusted to forefront*) without considering that whatever they are saying really does have merit as it relates to **you** (*or even that it has any kind of merit at all because if it is based on superficial or impractical concepts then most likely it's not in the best interest of anybody, which is why again you need to make sure that it does have validity before jumping on the bandwagon yourself*). And because of this is what you base your choices on as far as who you choose as a **mate** (*or mates because in situations like this marrying multiple times can now become part of the norm especially if a person's physical attributes is primarily what you are focusing on when deciding to marry; whether it be going outside of your race just to have what you now feel is prime time material or even from within it, where your criteria is still again based on the mainstream's point of view with this person being a black version of our white counterparts*), **career** (*with what others see as respectable occupations versus what is considered not, like jobs that require a college degree and those that don't with it again saying as it relates to the latter what you are looked upon as being as is who you are; with the biggest problem being with this kind of belief system is that it is based on the have/ have not philosophy with that of the former being able to say that they are better than someone else. Remember positive earning power is positive earning whether it be wearing a suit* *and tie or sweated jeans and a tee shirt, as long as it's a honest days work, who cares, a point that definitely is aim toward those who feel that sweeping floors or handling garbage is degrading, remember somebody's got to do it, with us ALL needing to show appreciation to those who have chosen to.) Getting too caught up on class issues is something we can't as black people afford and putting on airs because you have a little more education than someone else means nothing (unless you are truly running things and not just a puppet on somebody else's string) if you still find yourself in the position of having the rug pulled out from under you just like in the same way it can happen to those you are looking down on. Even though you have more options than a person who doesn't have a degree there's always the danger of you becoming complacent under the thinking that you have arrived where because of this you fall into the trap of letting your guard down with you becoming a little slack, a point that'll be further discussed later on; with you also understanding that the last hired first fired policy still applies to you regardless of how qualified or proficient you are on the job; something if you don't believe me just look at the unemployment line with it being mostly us on it.);* **and** more importantly just how you live your **life** *(with you taking on attitudes and value systems of the mainstream without making sure that even they themselves are on the right track, remember white folks live for the thrill of it all with them not always looking before they leap so jumping in the fire with them is not necessarily in our best interest all the time with the consequences being that much more greater if what they are doing turns out to be another foolish endeavor because where they may be able to bounce back* *from their actions we may not simply on the bases of who we are).* **Ok** now getting to the heart of all that's wrong with what's just been mentioned is you not having a clear understanding as to how you should be seeing **things** (*something occurring from constantly being under the thumb of others; with those desiring to be accepted feeling that their only option out* (*you know like with you taking the "if you can't beat them, join them" stance*) *is to fall in line with you doing exactly what you think they want us to do something creating a state of gullibility*) **something** again causing you to miss the boat of opportunity that would have been available to you if you had chosen to see the possibilities (*by being placed in a situation that is designed specifically for you*) from not being true to yourself with it also further delaying your journey to contentment from a restless spirit and what I mean by this is suppose you had succeeded in getting what those consider to be the desired lifestyle; something where you marry the beautiful girl with a great job thrown in there based on you having all the educational credentials needed; living in the best neighborhood with your kids going to the best schools. Sounds pretty good, huh, except in your relationship where your wife is overly consumed with making a name for herself by trying to keep up with not only the Jones but the Steinman's, Brockman's, and Ford's as well with you working your butt off just to support her extravagant shopping habit, because after all the only reason you married her was for the perks of having a show piece on your arm (*or similar philosophies where getting ahead becomes the ultimate goal*). Now as far as your kids are concerned with them being the only blacks in their school they are also forced to have to adapt; something causing them to completely abandon everything having to do with their cultural with your daughter wearing contact lenses and acting like she can use the same hair products as her white counterparts instead of what she should be using for maintaining her hair due to her not wanting to be an outcast from having to explain to her friends why she can't use theirs. With your son, desiring to also fit in, refusing to understand what driving while black means with him being in denial when he hears about his cousin from the other side of town being harassed by the cops for being in your neighborhood. Lastly since all the guys at work are involved in extra-martial affairs you figure why can't you with you and your secretary hitting it too. Now if you don't get how all this mess could eventually blow up in your face (*with you despising the man you've become*), then I don't know what else to say; oh yeah something else I forgot to mention is you really never wanted to be in the corporate environment anyway but instead a teacher, however because of the full ride you received that enabled you to go to a prestigious college with the general consensus being from all those putting their two cents in that it would be a shame to waste this kind of opportunity on something that doesn't bring about as much clot as well, lets say like an executive would which is why when you went away you broke up with the girl who you really had something in common with because she was a little too down for your new found friends taste (*something again explaining why you are cheating on your wife now with you trying to fill the void left from not having nothing more in common with her than mutual materialistic aspirations*). Of course a lot of you might say what is the point of this example as it relates to this current discussion, well what I wanted to show you is how when you allow what others see as being success can sometimes work against you if you don't have a good understanding on what's important and by not looking before you leap with you desiring to be accepted in a society that pretty much rejects all of who you are I hope I am painting a picture as to what can happen under circumstances like this; with it again all saying why you need to have a strong spiritual foundation with you basing your decisions on how things are really suppose to **be** (*like knowing your purpose with it again being important to understand that when you are not living the life Yah placed you on this earth for, you will always be left feeling unsettled; something bringing about a whole new set of problems just to cope, with you resorting to unscrupulous methods (like undercutting another just to get ahead through deception or mistreatment) or turning to destructive behavior (such as alcohol, drugs, abusive behavior (whether it be your spouse, children), infidelity, etc.);* **something** *that could save you a lot of time, aggravation and even tragedy (if any of the above resulted from it). One of the reasons why we as a people (meaning blacks folks) have such a difficult time adjusting to life outside of our own environment is from dealing with internal issues (like insecurities or doubt); something resulting from us listening to people in our camp who* *have a limited point of view as to what they see as being* **right** *(whether it be them either having no interest in or just not knowing how to get beyond their current circumstances. Ex. The play "A Raisin in the Sun" where the matriarch of the family, wanting to improve the conditions of her family, decides to move them out to a white neighborhood instead using their newfound windfall to better serve them in their own community, where they could have started a business that created an ongoing legacy for all concern; an example that I feel inspired the kind of exodus for other blacks following suit thereby manufacturing the very problems we have now, with those who have continually fought to fit in another's world and the have nots sinking under never ending despair from no longer having positive support systems.)* **or** *others outside of it with us opting to take what we feel is the best alternative following their lead (something that may not necessarily garner peace from possibly having to compromise just for the sake of getting ahead). And this is why getting lost in another's sauce of foolishness (or becoming envious of what we think we are missing out on) can lead to ruins with us now taking a step back instead of a step forward. Another problem coming out of this relates to the interracial dating issues where because again of black folks allowing themselves to be brainwashed into believing that anyone other than us is better, with black men, in particular, crossing racial lines, just to obtain what they think will elevate them (or bring to the table something we can't or won't bring) in someway. Now before I get into this, a point needs to be made here about black women not being supportive, loving or respectful to our men, with my personal feeling being that yes, in some cases I do agree with me seeing* *where you are coming from because like in any group there are those who exist that harbor some of these same traits so of course there's a strong possibility that some of you may run into a few sisters who have no interest in standing by their man with them just only being interested in going for self or just wanting to be in control, however it is also important to remember that if you, yourself are* **superficial** *(or not very discerning when it comes to recognizing who's real and who isn't, or who has a loving spirit versus a confrontational one)* **then** *the likelihood of you coming up short is something you should be expecting to happen with it all saying that before you as black men start generalizing (with you putting all of us in the same bag) you should do some soul searching first making sure that you're not your own worst enemy (or even getting back what you send out to the universe); also from this knowing that there is a big ole world out here with there being plenty of other black women in other countries outside of the* **US** *(or even just outside of your immediate environment with you understanding that you may not find what you are looking for in your own back yard with you also understanding when you restrict yourself to just the familiar all you are doing is nothing more than recycling it; with you constantly running into the same kind of personality over and over again) that operate under different concepts than what you have probably already experienced (something to think about as this also applies to* BLACK WOMEN *as well); with you understanding that broadening your horizons is not just limited to going outside of your race to find someone but to other cultures as well. Ok now with that out of the way let's get back to the business at hand with us discussing the dangers of choosing your mates by others'* *standards. Again there are various reasons why you as brothers would consider dating those of another color with the only valid one being is love (with everything else eventually falling apart). As it relates to this section though (with the others being discussed later), again how you see yourself is how you see others of the same so if you feel less than, your desire to seek those out not that of yourself is what you will go for, with the problem simple being* YOU NOT LOVING YOURSELF, *which means with any relationship you pursue there are going to be problems. And by basing things on others' standards who go along with this, you will find yourself never being truly satisfied because there will always be fault with those you choose to love; with you setting yourself up to be proven* **wrong** *(one of the things I love about our Father is how he finds creative ways of getting his point across with him using our own stupidity to do it)* **because** *again you are working off the philosophy that something is wrong with black women in general when that may not be the* **case** *(outside of being human, something we all are with you not expecting anything more of us than what you'd be expecting from them).* **There** *is nothing wrong with being drawn to a person because of certain attributes as long as it is based on genuine* **admiration** *(or taste, a circumstance where motives are absence from the decision) with the problem being when it* **isn't** *(and you finally realizing this as you now become more comfortable in your own skin)* **you'll** *have to live with the fact that you might've been bypassing those without merit who would have been far better suited for you (from having similar experiences) with you wasting yours as well as the ones you've been pursuing time from not having the proper perspective (great lesson learned,* *huh?). Something else to be aware of here is just like someone else was able to transfer their energy of superficial ness onto you with them making you feel inadequate you can easily do the same to others you **encounters** (ex. black women constantly seeing you with women of other races (or near white black versions of them) with them now in turn doubting themselves; something that could lead them to making unnecessary changes just to appease unrealistic expectations (with me saying shame on you). Something explaining why we're having a difficult time getting past this inferiority complex issue imposed on us by others with there still existing a great wedge between us and those seen as being the favored ones). **Side** note: To all black women out there, being superficial will get you no where when it comes to finding a man, because part of the reason for brothers jumping ship isn't always from them being unreasonable all the time but from our tripping over things that really don't amount to a hill of beans. One of the major complaints black men have concerning why they are choosing to be with women of other races is due to us blowing them off, with us putting some of them down for not being attractive enough, not having their plan in **place** (or so we say where they actually do with it just being from our own lack of vision that we don't recognize it) **with** them still working on it, or just being a little too corny for our taste (something adding to the fire in creating low self-esteem with everything I'm currently talking about resulting from it). However when things start taking off for them (or they have now finally come into their own) is when suddenly now interest on our part comes into play with it being too late because someone else seeing their potential has already made themselves at home with them* *having no intentions in vacating the premises. Again now mind you as I have been saying throughout this text that I do feel brothers should be working on getting themselves together first before pursuing romantic endeavors, however though, when they see us chasing behind their boys simply on the bases of their appearance or so-called* **Swag** *(something that should be looked upon as only being the icing on the cake with it again being considered nothing but fluff, with it leaving us empty if that's all they have to offer),* **anyone** *would be scratching their heads wondering why can't they get some love too. Remember nobody starts out the gate with everything in order (as we are all works in progress) so again before dissing a brother without first finding out what he's really about, keep in mind the ones we've already lost to the other team with us asking ourselves can we as black women really afford to lose anymore, think about it! And on that note continuing on with why you as black men can no longer allow others to define your manhood with you understanding that because we have been placed in a no win situation where someone else is making the rules, with them being able to change the game as they see fit, puts you in the position of always having to jump through hoops. And again in saying that you have to be ok with the way in which you define yourself as a man. And what I mean by this is that you might not be bringing home the bigger check or able to run a company however as long as you are taking responsibility for your actions, know how to get in where you fit in with regards to how you relate to your* **woman** *(with you understanding if money is not her problem with her having her own, then your next course of action should be learning how to be more attentive to her emotionally where she will now look to you for*

STRENGTH, WISDOM, AND ENCOURAGEMENT, *as well as someone she can count on (or be the kind of companion that she can truly enjoy sharing her life with, etc.)),* **be** *an example to others in your community with them seeing that just because you don't walk around with a big stick you still have a right to be treated with respect; with you also showing that being a man is not limited to just financial or status motivating endeavors but by more tangible qualities with you knowing that it's not what you have that makes you a man but how you live your life with you making the best of whatever opportunities are available to you versus wimp'ng out because of what you think you lack in. Everyday we see numerous examples of those (whether they be young or old) we admire squandering their blessings from being irresponsible; a situation that brings about the question as to why do we as a society put so much emphasis on money and status when it comes to how we define men (especially when you look at our current state of affairs with those who do lacking in so many other ways) when it is very obvious that being one embodies so much more. And this is what I mean by not allowing others to define your manhood because what they may be basing things on will eventually mean nothing when the chips are really* **down** *(or all hell breaks loose where neither money nor position will get you out of anything, again Mr. Cosby, Tiger Woods, as well as those such as O.J. and the likes). Now the main reason for bringing this particular point up is because of the feelings of inadequacy black men are left with from them not always being the true breadwinners in the family with it causing major division between us and them (like of course you not being able to deal with us making more money than you or from those who* *do (like ball'ers, entertainers, etc.) with you being on a quest to maintain your position of headship by attempting to shutdown our continued desire of wanting to be independent, if that's what we were when you got with us (or squash it before we start thinking about doing our own thing) out of fear of being dethrone (or us no longer looking at you with the same reverence, something again that would never change if everything else is right with you being well rounded, dependable, loving, and true blue because even though financial security is important it isn't the whole story as to what makes a relationship, something being even more so now with our kids needing both parents actively participating in their lives which is why operating off the concept that bringing home the bacon is what all it's going to take will again eventually find you coming up short (again something I know already mentioned before but hey, you guys have got to understand that, baby, it really is a new day). Because in today's times with most black women being nothing less than self sufficient, we need a little more from our mates than what our mothers, grandmothers, or great-grandmothers once required))).*

b. The problem with allowing others to dictate your future from desiring to maintain the status quo by being complacent with you feeling that you have arrived and not being prepared when things fall apart. Here this point relates to us, as black folks, not reinvesting in our communities or having a back up plan just in case things take a turn for the worst. A lot of times when we have accomplished the goal of getting the ideal job, lifestyle, etc. we take the position of only desiring to maintain what we've gained with us forgetting that at any given time, the rug can still be pulled out from under us (*or again the last hired, first fired threat*). And without having a back up plan as well as the right people in your corner who would've supported you through the **storm** (*like a wife who marries you on the basis of more than what you financially bring to the table instead of the kind who most likely would be looking for greener pastures once you are no longer able to provide her with the lifestyle she is accustomed to*) **you** will fall flat on your butt. And unfortunately this is what happens when complacency meets arrogance with you feeling a little too comfortable for your own good being, in most cases, a disconnect occurring between where you are now and where you were before becoming a rising **star** (*or you living in never, never land from having a silver spoon in your mouth all your life, which could be even worst as you would be completely lost when reality finally hits; from not knowing what it's like to have never had*) with you turning your back on your **past** (*something usually occurring out of fear of losing what you've worked so hard to obtain as well as you again desiring to be part of the mainstream's team from the feeling that not achieving the American dream makes you less than those you admire; something again relating to all what has been discussed thus far*). **There** is a saying that goes "too much is given much is required" with you understanding that the blessings you've already received are not just for your sake but for the betterment of others; so when you no longer feel the need to relate to those from whence you came, you put yourself in the position of having to watch your back. The benefits of reinvestment are: Bridging the gap between the haves/ and have nots by making your presence known through mentorship or investment in other's ideas so they too could positively move forward; creating opportunities that could eventually lead you to completely being your own man with you literally running the show (*or creating joint ventures, where others like you would all collectively pool your resources together to start new business entities*); creating a safety net for yourself so that if things do fall apart for you on your end you'll have something to fall back **on** (*like if you move out of your old neighborhood with you still holding on to the home you once lived in (along with you possibly purchasing additional properties in that same area) as a way of helping to maintain a decent neighborhood (something where you could rent out to other family members, etc. or up and coming professionals, as a way of assuring that the integrity of that particular area stays in tact) or keeping abreast on what's going on with their educational system by becoming a board member; something allowing you to have a say on the running of these schools with you making sure that their standards are in line with everybody else's (something again in both cases would create a safety net for yourself as well as for your family because you never know if you have to go back there to live with you having to send your kids to these same schools or if one of your kids starts dating someone from the hood, with you not losing your mind that he or she may be behind from an academic standpoint; something which can also bring about room for concern when it comes to those who your kids might bring home with them being an even more gangster version of you (a, can we again say mentorship program* *please, yeah!*)). **Also** another aspect of this point is now how you again are allowing people like your mates and/or associates to influence you in such a way that they are able to discourage you from taking on projects of this **nature** (*even if it is seen as a possible business venture that could one day guarantee you life long security, with it also being something that could be passed down to future generations*) because of their own self absorbed **motives** (*like with your wife protecting her own interest from not understanding the importance of giving back or reinvestment*) **and** your associates not wanting to be reminded of their own lackings by keeping you in their fold. It's important to never sleep on the kinds of opportunities that allow you to be your own **man** (*with you knowing that taking the blessings that have been given to you with you in turn using them for the betterment of others can open up the possibilities in more ways than you'll ever imagine*).

c. Not being prepared to take on responsibilities as a man with you still looking at us to pick up the slack in the same way your momma would. Now just because your mother puts up with your foolishness, doesn't mean you should be expecting us to. Remember there is a difference between a mother's love and that of your woman with her being a nurturer and us being a **supporter** (*with us needing something to support, from you again having a plan in place; something being not the same as it relates to your mother because you already exist with it being again because of hers and your father's actions that you are here and what she's suppose to do, regardless of what's going on in your life*). **And by being** confused over the role of the other you think that you can lay up on us the same way you lay up on her (*even though you shouldn't be doing that either once you become an able bodied adult*). **Being** a man is not just based on what you are bringing sexually but on how you handle your business outside of the bedroom with you being able to take on life's day to day challenges. Again I'm not saying that you have to be bling, **blinging** (*of course if you pursue a person who expects this then you may have to make it do what it do by having good loot in your pockets*) but you should at least be able to hold your own with you properly assessing what you can and cannot do before stepping to a **person** (*something again called discernment or wisdom, with it being us seeing that you have some sense we will follow*). **Expecting** us to live off the hope that you are going to get it together eventually is like stringing us along especially if we're talking indefinitely. (*And if you feel you need that kind of buying time then don't pursue us until things are where they should be with you again using discernment when choosing someone instead of jumping at every opportunity that comes your way with you trying to impress them with what you now have young whipper snapper; something when it does happen could bring about disillusionment with you complaining about how she is playing you like a dummy*). Because what you are attempting to do when desiring us to wait for you like this is trying to get something for nothing (*or a definite maybe*) with you putting us in the position of having to compromise ourselves; something where we could be left holding the bag if things don't come into fruition (*or if you decide to* *move onto greener pastures yourself*); which again is why I'm bringing it up with me wanting you to realize how unfair you are being with the true motivation from this is you just being selfish (*and dead wrong with you putting cart before the horse*) as this is really more about you wanting to get your penis **serviced** (*something where though you have regard for your goals and desires there seems to be very little for ours (with there also being a very obvious lack of regard for our virtue as well with you treating us like sex objects*), **and** by doing so I have to wonder how can you say this is love when we are the ones taking on the greatest amount of risk because after all we're working off of your maybe remember; something where you, yourself are not completely sure how this is going to play out. Understanding that part of loving someone isn't about just you getting something out of the deal but us as well with the only way this situation being somewhat feasible is if we volunteer (*with us both being realistic about what may or may not happen*) to wait for you and not from you asking something like that of **us** (*now I know a lot of you like to look at this as us being down for you but whether you realize it or not you are creating an even more insecure environment with us constantly being plagued with doubt because of it (a, do I say future pressure on you my brother with you having to deal with a woman's scorned if things don't work out; something explaining why (when again things do go sour) we are able to get a piece of your pie during the divorce from all the loving support WE provided while you were pursuing your goals.*)). **Because** black men are so use to getting sex they look at it as some kind of entitlement with you working off the thought processes that you don't have to be responsible. With the problem also being here is you feeling that you don't have to do anymore than what you are currently doing (*being complacent*) with you never looking to better **yourself** (*which for young men now coming up this seems to be the route they are taking more and more, however, if we as women chose not to accept this kind of stance from the onset where these brothers are again now forced to deal with the realities of no romance without having something actually in* **place** (*like the kind of job that sustains more than one with the possibility of a future* **existing** (*something you may say but what if that it is the best they can do, then I suggest you only pursue young ladies who are willing to work with* **you** (*and there are some POSITIVE* **BEAUTIFUL** *black women out* **there** **(you know with the kind of physical attributes you like, something that when you think otherwise is you again generalizing, that only the least attractive will have your back)** **who** *will do that where you both can now slowly built a decent life for yourselves together*) **with** *you again willing to pick up the slack in other departments instead of continually copping out or allowing yourself to get caught up in negative endeavors where now moving forward becomes that much more difficult if you ever choose to do so*) **and** *them being mature enough to take on real responsibilities*) **they** *might opt to stay in school with them working a little harder on getting a few things accomplished first*); **something** that throws us all under the bus with the vicious cycle of foolishness **continuing** (*you know like unwanted children that you can't take care of or infidelities because of you not* *truly being ready to settle down, etc.*) with you expecting us (*because again of you seeing momma doing it*) **to** pick up the slack. (SIDE NOTE: FOR THOSE WHO DISAGREE WITH WHAT I'M SAYING HERE, I HAVE ONE QUESTION TO ASK, WHICH IS WAS YOUR MOM (*SINCE THIS IS THE EXAMPLE YOU ARE BASING YOUR CHOICES ON*) HOLDING THINGS DOWN ALONE WHILE YOU WERE COMING UP OR WAS YOUR FATHER STILL IN THE PICTURE; SOMETHING IF HE WASN'T (*FROM HIM NOT BEING ALL THE MAN HE SHOULD BE*) OBVIOUSLY INDICATES THAT IT DIDN'T WORK FOR HER SO WHY IS IT GOING TO WORK FOR US (*WITH AGAIN HISTORY BEING REPEATED*), NOW THERE! A POINT MENTIONED EARLIER WITH ONLY A SMALL MINORITY BEING LUCKY ENOUGH TO FIND A PERSON WHO THEY CAN DO THIS WITH) Now as far as you getting involved with women who don't want anything, you have to have enough for yourself to stand your ground with you not allowing others to distract you from your goals, something which if you choose to do this, you'll eventually regret once you realize how hard it is to get back on track again; that's why knowing that there are other fish in the sea works in your favor with there being even more opportunities awaiting you just in case your current situation doesn't work out; and by not allowing others to bring you down because of their own lack of vision (*or insecurities*) you now have the chance of becoming the man you were destined to be with you possibly choosing someone in the future who compliments you instead of ones who want to control you by acting like your mother.

d. Continuation of (c) now it may take a village to raise a child but that still doesn't mean you are off the hook when it comes to your own personal responsibilities with you understanding why you shouldn't be looking to create these additional responsibilities (*children*) if you are not going to be there for them. Throughout the years of slavery and Jim Crow as well as from the effects of the welfare system during the sixties, seventies, and eighties (*where a large number of men were encourage not to stay in the home in order for women to continue receiving federal support*) you have pretty much been nothing more than sperm donors with you either not being able to be a father to your children or just choosing not to, something that now naturally seems to be part of your MO with you easily being able to do it without too much guilt, however, continuing to create children, with you knowing that you had no intentions of sticking around is almost criminal. Again if you are not interested in being more than what you are because of your own lack of self-worth then don't put those who are only here because of your desire to get yours through this; with you again thinking that other family members, your child's mother, or sociality as a whole is going to pick up the pieces you left behind. Just because certain conditions were imposed on you doesn't justify the crime anymore nor does it (*if you do decide to stick around*) give you the right to pass on bad concepts to your offsprings with them also now feeling inferior. Look at all the children left behind who have been abused, or emotionally damaged from them wondering why their fathers just didn't want to be part of their **lives** (*or even if they did, because of their own problems, they don't have the ability to do the right thing* (*like fight for their kids*) *from not having a leg to stand on*). **Being** a single mother myself I know my daughter wishes her father had been around; and with me again knowing that it's a void I just couldn't fill, I feel even stronger about this particular issue because of it not being fair to her. No matter how much you may've been led into believing that you aren't important and that your children will be ok whether you are in the home or not, you can't count on others to do what you could've done if you were. And why I hope that you as black men will eventually find a way to make this thing called life work where now you can be what all we need you to be instead of continuing behavior that leaves nothing but loose ends for someone else to try to mend back together again or them just always remaining that way with your child never feeling quite whole because of it. Side note: Questions to you mothers out there. Are you, as black women raising your sons to be the man he is suppose to be or just to be your surrogate **man** (*even if there is a man in the house* (*like his father*) *where now the two are pitted against each other because of you babying your son and him just wanting the boy to grow up, with him wanting him to get his own women instead jacking his*) **with** you now finding yourself competing for his attention with the other woman (*or women*) who is suppose to be his mate, with him looking to replace you with her because of his desire to keep the party of dependency going (*something explaining why you are tripping*). Do you value men in general with your son knowing that he has worth or are you not only constantly putting men down with you transferring some of this resentment over to not only him but your daughter as well with her seeing men in this same way too (*and the vicious cycle continues*). Are you guiding him to his destiny or leading him away from it because of your own feelings of insecurities or lack of vision from you not seeing the possibilities **yourself** (*something explaining why we should value men a little more with them being able to provide the kind of support that motivates our young men to go out and get what's rightfully theirs just like in the same way a lion challenges his cub by toughening him up as well as awakening his thirst for adventure. Something with it again saying when their presence isn't there to help bring this about a void is created with them not knowing how to properly handle themselves much like the way a real man should where now they don't necessarily always understand the importance of duty or perseverance with them giving up all the time, as well as not learning how to better use logic (where they are now able to be the calm in the storm) instead emotion (something causing them to fly off the handle at times) when it comes to resolving conflicts*) **and** also by limiting his prospects you too are shooting yourself in the foot because when you think about how ball'ers, those in the entertainment field, etc., who in most cases, attribute what they've accomplished to their families with their mothers being prime recipients of this gratitude (*because of the love and guidance that was shown to them by her*) you realize why you should be helping to nurture their dreams instead of discouraging them. And lastly do you truly represent what he should be looking for in a woman with him understating the importance of having a balanced life just by the way how you live yours (*something relating to the first question*) and is the example you're setting, something that could possibly cause him to abandon ship just as his father did when he too encounters love.

e. All the other reasons black men choose to cross the line with him seeking women of other races out. Touching on this earlier from point (a) I felt there are a few more things that needed to be addressed as it relates to this particular subject. With some of the main ones stemming from you not wanting to hold your own as a man, with you again looking for us to carry you or attempting to keep us down with you; wanting us to compromise ourselves in someway (*with us crossing all moral boundaries, whether it be sexual, criminal, etc.*) or wanting us to put up with all the foolishness you can dish out, something where which I then suggest you keep on running to the boarder because no self respecting black woman would or should want to be bothered with that. Like I said earlier I know it's not always from you being unreasonable about certain things but us, however, what I'm talking about here is based on you expecting us to jump through hoops just to appease your again foolish indulgences; something which makes you not even worth the first initial look. And why we would be better off without you because after all we do know to how to do this ourselves with you missing the boat from all we have to offer, _____ (*be my guess and fill that one in*). Another thing with this is if you are operating off the concept that the benefits from associating with those outside of our race are far **better** (*something where you are looking just to get ahead (or that you see as having a better value system)*), than with those who look like you, you might be sadly disappointed when you find out otherwise that it doesn't with it working more against you if those you are trying to impress are either not amused by this (*with them being envious*) or because of the general consensus being from even her own people that she is nothing more to talk about than what you think you are avoiding us **for** (*like with her being more trashy than classy, something where if being the case with there also being a definite pattern already established from those you've previously dated before as well (with them also having similar characteristics) might be more of an indication of the kind of women you are naturally drawn to than anything else with again the point being that you might need to do a little soul searching here with you understanding that no matter what the flavor (vanilla, caramel, chocolate, etc.) you can't get gold out of silver*); **what** do you do now, when you are being laugh at more than respected for this decision with the reason behind what I am currently saying due to you judging others (*as well as generalizing with you only seeing your own one way*) with you again needing to understand that operating off of the philosophy on who you think is the better choice (*with it again being based on what the mainstream deems valid*) doesn't always guarantee promotion; with the issue being for me here is because of racism we as black women have an excuse for some of our discrepancies; as I, as well as, other inquiring minds, would like to know what's theirs since everything about them is suppose to be all good, but I guess in your self loathing eyes even the least of them is better than the best of us, huh? And in cases where you are seen as stepping on **toes** (*like getting with what our oppressors consider to be prime time and them desiring that person too; something that might put you in grave danger with these same people deciding to move you completely out of the way and by any means necessary if they have to. Which explains why you do usually end up with their throwaways as this becomes all that is available to you; an outcome that puts you exactly where you didn't want to be which is being associated with a so called nobody* (*and what I consider to be an example of what bad karma looks like*)). **The** last thing coming out of pursuing women like this is you constantly going from person to person until you run out of options; something again being your choice if you continue on this path with you understanding that every dog has his **day** (*with you actually getting yours, since that was originally the intent because of your desiring to benefit at another's expense*). **Outside** of being arrogant or just plain lazy, some of you do this because of you not believing in yourself with you now looking for others who allow you to control them in this way; with this actually being the reason for you seeking those of other ethnic persuasions out because again you already know that most black women who've accomplished a few things are just not willing to put up with this kind of trifle-ness. Something which, like I said earlier is fine however, it's important to remember that EVERYBODY has limits with those you feel you could get over on tiring of such mistreatment themselves with them eventually moving on as well and again why when it is all said and done just doing the right thing by being the man you're suppose to be as well as cleansing yourself of beliefs that it is ok to devalue and/or use anyone for any **reason** (*something usually occurring from you either experiencing hurt yourself or just from your upbringing with you seeing this kind of behavior growing up*) **is** really best with you now garnering the kind of options where you won't have to take the easy way out; with you again bringing things to the table that adds to the relationship instead of looking to benefit without the other person involved not, from constantly taking away from it.

Something to ponder, first to my Caucasian brothers and sisters, why do trip so hard (*or get so offended*) when we choose to participate in activities that celebrate our culture, (*like Black Expos, Unity festivals etc.*) when you have things such as Greek and October Fest, St. Patrick Day, etc. I mean like what's wrong with us acknowledging things that relate to us in the same manner in which you do with you being able to still continue traditions from that of your beginnings. And the reason for me bringing this up is because I was reading a blog about one of our events (*the Black Expo*) with a white person writing in asking why do we still have them and what if white folks decided to do the **same** (*with me responding by saying you do, with the situation being in either case neither race is excluded from that of the other's with it being you just choosing not to participate, so there; something being not our* (*or black folks*) *problem*). **Now** for us, since other groups do have areas designated in cities across the land like "Little Italy, China Town, German Town, etc., where not only are these cultures celebrated but also enjoy economic benefits where products relating to their culture are sold with those on the outside seeking them out as well, what if we as a race also had TRUE designated areas throughout the country bringing together not only just the Black American experience, but African as well as Caribbean/Latin American cultures, giving a haven to artists, shops, businesses, theaters, eateries, educational **programs** (*with us all having access to historical information relating to these cultures where INDEPT history would be available with those coming from these areas actually facilitating them* (*something again where not only would our youth benefit from the educational aspect* (*language, customs, etc.*) *of this but others as well*)), and uniquely designed housing representing these **cultures** (*where a student exchange program could also be incorporated*), etc. (*do I see economic development for up and coming professionals and those looking for investment ventures as well as a possible way of bringing different cultural groups* (*African and Caribbean*) *together where we could have international festivals in those locales as well where the sharing of ideas could be achieved with it giving us the ability to reconnect on a much broader scale*). **Now** again the reason for bringing this up is though we do have businesses that carter to our culture, they all seem to be so spread out (*in different location, like the suburbs*) that only a few have access to them or if they are in the city they are so obscured that they are almost invisible. So by doing something like this with it being in a concentrated area that (*and because of the nature of the community*) could be looked upon as being an true economic Mecca where now we might value it enough to keep it up with others also desiring to support it. Another issue from this is with us being so quick to dismiss our own culture for someone else's we miss the opportunity to command our ship with us constantly being at the mercy of others. (*Side note: To all of you who feel that I am leaning toward being a segregationist, something to keep in mind here, there was a definite reasons why we were in Africa (just like those who came from Asia or Europe) with it being important to understand that what works for one group may not necessarily work for another (ex. the foods we've been eating since arriving in this country versus what we ate while we were still in our native land, something that might be better suited for us, where now because of us digesting things considered foreign could possibly be causing us greater harm than good with us being exposed to illnesses we might not have otherwise been exposed to (something that even white folks need to heed to as well especially in regards to sitting out in the sun just for the sake of getting a tan, where the possibility of developing skin cancer is now greater; remember there is a reason you are white with you coming from the kind of climates that accommodates these attributes), with the same being when it comes to how we now manage our hair, etc.) so by learning more about our culture with us getting back to basics could, in the long run, be more beneficial to our well being.*) Additional side note here, as it relates to the Black man/woman issue with both parties attempting to fit in; with Black men desiring women of other hues, and Black women not necessarily being able to complete, a lot of Black men would say, since we believe they should be able to financially hold their own much in the same way as our White counterparts, they of course feel justified in their quest for what is considered to be the best with the problem being here is that it is much easier for a person to create opportunities for themselves (such as through entrepreneurship, entertainment, etc., hard work with advancement now being made available) than it is to re-create oneself to fit another's standard of beauty without possible physical harm being done, something all saying that what Black men are asking or desiring is not only unreasonable but again an ultimate slap in Yah's face; with you also needing to remember that He ordained men to be providers with him not requiring anyone whether male or female to be anything other than what he designed them to be.

In reference to the previous chapter as well as the "Lust vs Insecurity" section of "The Men Issues" chapter, the following are examples of what vision and drive looks like where through them black men have either moved on from negative **circumstances** (*creating opportunities for themselves - Michael Cole, coming out of prison with him starting his Mickey Likes It ice cream joint and his product now being serve in places such as Jay-Z's 40/40 clubs; with another storyline being a group of young men out of Baltimore who also started their own ice cream company "Food for Thought" with the mission being that of wanting to create social change in their community, where through crowdfunding The Taharka Brothers, were able to buy their own truck for the distribution of their product*) **or** inspired by showing those working off limited concepts another way (*From stories by filmmakers One9 and Erik Parker where the telling of how Nas's 1994 classic Illmatic was made have helped to demonstrate that by making the best of what's available to you at the time (resources outside of the school system) one can still move forward with ones goals with it possibly taking you even more further than preferred methods (**formal education**); something being though someone such as Nas didn't complete H.S., he, along with his brother, still continued the process of learning through the reading of books supplied by their musician father; and all explaining his lyrical content with him being one of hip hop's most respected MCs of our time*). And with there being countless other testimonies outside of the ones mentioned, it is easy to see that when you believe it you can achieve it once you find your voice (*or purpose*) in this game called life.

Reader's Notes

Reader's Notes

Reader's Note

Reader's Notes

Chapter Six

Gay Issues

Hey, just had to ask . . . .

Understanding I'm about to tread in dangerous territory by the mere mention of homosexuality, however, since I talked about everything else, I figured why not and with me bringing up a few points to ponder, I just had to ask . . . .

Now with all the for and against arguments out there concerning whether we should live and let live; something to a certain extent may really be our only recourse because individually, we all will eventually be taken to task on the way in which we have chosen to live our lives with Yah having the final say as to what he deems acceptable (*something we as humans need to come to grips with*). And with us as heterosexuals being out of order ourselves, how can we expect anybody else to respect our Father's directives when we already don't. Wanting others to curtail their behavior all while we continue being foul will only foster resistance, and in saying that it becomes very clear that it starts with us as then maybe those seen as operating outside the box will also become more accepting of society's stance against what most view as wrong. Now of course the danger in choosing to continue on this seemingly unconcerned path (*from again not wanting to adhere to the rules ourselves*) the question now again becomes how far are we willing to push the envelope? Because once full acceptance on this particular issue occurs what's **next** (*sex with anything and everything available to us or breaking every commandment mentionable, something of course that kind of sounds like the start of total anarchy*) **and** this is my first "just had to ask" point to ponder. A point that is constantly missed with us not understanding **that** (*as it relates to our flesh*) in order to move closer to Yah (*FROM THE WEDGE THAT WAS CREATED BECAUSE OF ADAM AND EVE, DISOBEYING HIM INITIALLY* (*something which we see where it got them* (*kicked out of the Garden of Eden with the curse of sin becoming part of their makeup as well as future generations thereafter*))) we are suppose to be working on cleansing ourselves of what we desire to indulge in instead of giving into it with us demonstrating to our Father that we love him more than that, which will eventually pass. And by choosing something that really doesn't make or break us we are giving it more validity than it deserves. I mean really people it is only **sex** (*except in cases where self-loathing is involved where a person no longer wants to be identified in their natural state, with them changing their whole being* (*a point discussed a little later*)) **not** food or water (*something if when deprived of will create a life threatening situation*) with it really being not worth all the risk (*from desiring to pervert its purpose*) when you think about it and how it leads to eternal damnation from you continuing to disobey. A lot of us forget we are here for our Father's will with him already knowing how the plan is suppose to play out, so he will allow us, to go through a few things in order to get us on the right track (*or to impress upon us whatever point he needed to be made across*) it's just when we decide to go our own way is when things get sticky and what widens the gap that much more between us and him. My next point to ponder is the self acceptance issue with me wanting to know if you can't accept all of who you are yourself then why expect anybody else to only accept what you desire to put out there. Now what I mean by this is though there are many **circumstances** (*self hatred, gender envy, forced influential intrusion* (*something where* *because of certain behavior or physical traits a person exhibits, others impose what they think you should be thereby coercing you to make changes that probably would not have normally occurred, if you had been left alone) etc.)* **that** can cause a person to change the natural order of things by restructuring the dynamics of who they are, however, again no matter the reasoning behind this is, one thing here's for certain you are definitely spitting again in Yah's face with the question being what are you going to say to him when the time of final judgment is upon us *(with another question to ponder here being why is it ok to reinvent oneself as it relates to sexual identity goes but when it comes to racial ones, those who attempt to alter their features from skin bleaching and/or plastic surgery, are called out in abundance; something that comes across as being pretty hypocritical on society's part if you ask me with it being the same difference).* Allowing the spirit of discontentment *(or even fear)* to take over with you now working off thought processes that say that it's ok to alter oneself *(or take the position that it is ok to be what you are not)* is detrimental; with me also wanting to know why is it so difficult to marry internal likings with your external being. I mean a man can still be a man and appreciate his feminine side just like a woman can be a woman and still be able to appreciate certain aspects of her less feminine self without suppressing everything **else** *(something of course outside of sexual endeavors, with procreation being its main purpose; something that can only come about with what is opposite of you (something which again for me is another problem I have with this lifestyle, with you desiring what is unnatural until you decide to create life and that's when you need a man's sperm or a woman's egg and womb to achieve the goal of having a child* **(hum interesting))**. Then there is the issue of you again not *desiring that of your opposite with you being drawn to those like you who alter themselves to be what you say don't want (with me again still saying really?).* **Something** explaining why we as heterosexuals question the validity of your stance with me again just wanting to know if you desire that of who you are but in it's unnatural form then what's the point. I mean I can respect those who at least stay true to the game by being who they are with them desiring those who do the same, but the mere fact that what is opposite of you is what you still desire in someway makes very little sense, and what is even worst is those who have chosen to alter who they are taking on the worst characteristics of that which they say they don't desire with women acting like dogs as well as being abusive (*something occurring with you now being able to take your lover on in a way you couldn't do with a man*) or men being just as deceitful, petty, and conniving as a woman would be (*again really?*) something I guess being based on the behavior of those they desire to emulate with them seeing this as a way of gaining the advantage, or again the oppressed becoming the oppressor with them treating others they way in which they once were treated. And what I feel is more about gender envy with it being due to some lackings in their emotional being where certain events had to have occurred in their life earlier with them not addressing it **properly** (*like with them going through a true healing process that would have allowed them to get to the heart of the matter instead masking the pain by taking on attributes of those who they feel hurt them in this way (or because of what they see as being admiral qualities like in the case of a young man having no respect for other men in general (something that may've resulted from possibly hurt inflicted on him from abuse or abandonment) with* *instead him desiring to be more like the women around him), with you also deciding that you would rather do what is pleasing in Yah eyes versus what is not. Again a lot of us want to place blame on our Father for things that circumstances itself brought on with you not looking at the person (or persons) who really did this to you with you knowing that they didn't operate in accordance to how they were truly suppose to behaved. Remember we are all given free will with us usually taking liberty to do as we please (something causing us to fall short by either not holding up our end of the bargain (from not taking responsibility for our actions) or being completely disobedient)) where now innocent people are put in unwelcoming situations, (like mental and physical abuse) or lack of acceptance (from them desiring to do things or having interest that are seen as being opposite of the norm like young men wanting to pursue dance or young ladies pursuing certain sports; something in both cases that can leave them vulnerable to another's deceptive concepts). Side note here for gay men who are completely out, if you are dealing with a down low brother, how can you really trust him to do the right thing by you if he can't even be honest about his sexuality with those outside of you, with it being if he was HIV would he tell you, and if he is cheating on his woman with you how do you know he is not cheating on you with others (another issue you'd probably have to contend with since most men have a problem with monogamy anyway), with you remembering that a dog is a dog no matter the flavor. Now for women, though HIV has been mostly associated with homosexual activity it is important to remember that the real culprit here is promiscuous behavior and by saying this don't always assume that your man is gay (or gay-ist from thinking that he might be going both ways) because of his status but instead it being more about him being irresponsible as well as disrespectful to your relationship by being sexually involved with ANYONE else other than you, because after all he can contract this disease from women (as well as sources involving blood contamination from dirty needles, etc.) and if we are talking about black women in particular the risk is that much more with us having a higher rate of HIV than most. Now the biggest problem with associating HIV with being gay is if your partner contracts it, he might be afraid to get tested because of the stigma (of being homosexual) attached to it; something that makes you that much more accessible to it also) Side note: With me directing this question to black women, who choose to emulate men. Knowing how they are negatively targeted, why would you want to wear their armor by trying to be like them; from threat of extinction through internal and external violence, to just being looked upon as menaces to society, what is gained from this behavior and what happens if you are truly taken seriously where now you are treated in the manner in which they are, just another had to ask question I wanted to put out there.).* **Now** my next point to ponder is for those who say you were born like this, ok well if that is truly the case, why are you recruiting then by taking advantage of those at their weakest moment? I mean why Yah does what he does with you being born this way *(just like how we all as humans harbor some kind of affliction),* to me, has always been about giving those not like this naturally the ability to know that if you can get through the storm they can too, however the problem comes in when you who were born into this again decided to take liberty with you even going so far as trying to bring others into the fold; something which is just plain criminal, with it again discrediting your stance because if you can recruit somebody into something you can pray yourself out of **it** *(example— Donnie McClurkin, who at one time was living a gay lifestyle, made a decision to turn over a new leaf by choosing to please Yah instead* *continuing to indulge his flesh, something where now people in that community are up in arms about, with me asking why, but of course I guess if the goal is to spread propaganda, arguments showing otherwise work more against you than for you, huh).* **Now** for kids who are looking for acceptance from their families (*again what you do once you are on your own is between you and Yah with him having the last word when final judgment takes place*), **putting** others in the position of compromising their values just to make you feel better is just selfish with it also coming across like as if you are having a temper tantrum if those you desire to give in don't. With me saying if this lifestyle is so important to you, take a stand by working your way to adulthood first so you can live your life as you **please** (*I mean because if this is truly who you are then nothing is going to change if you wait for the time when you can live your life on your own terms, right*) **as** you stand on your own two feet. Because expecting your parents (*or other love ones*) to accept what they really don't have to and all while you're under their roof is beyond disrespectful and by threatening to do harm to yourself is well just humm . . . . Desiring the approval of those you love is understandable, however, what you are talking about here is not a game, but a life altering decision, something that should happen when you are truly an adult who has come into their own, because in a lot cases, with most teens basing things on emotions rather than consequence, situations may **change** (*something if it doesn't with you still feeling this way after getting out on your own, you have a better leg to stand on as far as your parents respecting the fact that you are not subjecting them to this under their care.*) **where** if you decide later that this is not the direction you want to go into, you can avoid the drama you would have incurred if you attempted to tackle this issue earlier, something with me again giving you something else to ponder (*Additional side note here as it relates to black kids headed in this direction, with racial issues still being as they are, places them in a more detrimental position, from not only being unprepared when sexual identity is not a concern, but even more so when they are with opportunities even less available to them; and why I feel things of this nature should be postpone until they are fully establish.*) Getting into another of my just had to ask questions, is what if we all desired to go this way with Yah deciding (*because of this*) to take away our ability to access others of the opposite sex as **punishment** (*because again after all we are attempting to reject what he put in place by choosing to go in a different direction*); **something** that would stop procreation, with me wanting to know how long do you think we as the human race would last and for me this is one of the most crucial questions of them all because it shows how much we need each other as men and women with us again **needing** (*something obviously stemming from us easily discarding each other with us treating the other like an after thought*) **to** really understand the importance of why we are here. So when we try to pervert sex's purpose, replacing it with our fleshly desires, it can lead to dire consequences. Again each of us are made up of both male and female **genetics** (*remember again it requires both to create life*) **so** it is possible that an imbalance could occur, however that doesn't give us the right to overrule what Yah's preordained us to **be** (*I mean if you came out a boy then you are a boy and if you came out a girl you are a girl*) **something** where we should be looking to commit to it more with us loving ourselves completely as we truly are and not just the part we only want to accept, again just something to ponder. Now before bringing this to a close, I wanted to get into a few more "just had to ask" questions . . . . like for men, you do know that women can do all that a man can do and even more with the same being for women as it relates to men and what they can do for us; something that causes me to scratch my head as to why would anyone want to be bothered with the artificial when the real thing is so much better; or as it relates to the prison system where both men and women come back with additional options from either loneliness or repeated attacks with them now **desiring** (*or emotionally scarred with their outlook now being tainted*) **what** is perverted, something again that causes me to ponder as to how long are we as a society going to continue being ok with this and if **we** (*meaning black folks, since we seem to be the hardest hit with a lot of our people going to jail in record numbers*) **will** ever start demanding for the kind of prison reforms that would try to incorporate **discipline** (*during their stint where keeping themselves would be made easier through safety (for the purpose of minimizing rapes)*) **or** programs that help those who aren't coping well in this restricted environment to better deal with this situation, something that in turn could aid in reducing some of their anxieties of being incarcerated for long periods of **time** (*or vulnerable to this foolishness, because again remember the person coming to see them is waiting as they too have to deal with temptation rearing its ugly head also, so why can't those who are now incarcerated*) **as** well as finding ways to keep families in tact where when these people finally get out they would be able to create healthy relationships on the outside; with us all understanding that punishing them shouldn't mean that we as a society should continue suffering as well from these people now being even more worst off than when they went in initially, and lastly while we as women are so down with the plan by indulging our male gay friends, do you realize you are fraternizing with the enemy, I mean if they are trying to jock what you are trying to jock in the same way other women are doing then what's the difference, with me also wanting to know what are you thinking, cause if you are so concerned about one (*meaning women*) why not the other cause after all competition is **competition** (*side note: As women we need to keep in mind that there is a reason men are men and women are women, so when you desire our men to be more like us aren't you disrupting the natural order of things, with you eventually regretting it when you really need him to step up and not run for cover from him no longer knowing how to truly hold it down (or him being too much of a good thing where now there is no balance with us not having a true man's perspective, instead of one who is always cosigning). Also to women who got a man, why don't you walk a mile in the shoes of those who don't then come back and tell us how that worked for you with you still being sympathetic to those who choose to take on attributes similar to yours (or ole so accepting of this kind of behavior; and what I take such great offense to from knowing that we as women were created for the purpose of being a man's true compliment with us now being regulated out by someone else's design) from realizing the reduced number of men that are now available to date, and with you also again now understanding why you have to keep a reign on yours, think about it. Additional Side note here: Recently Jada Picket-Smith posed a question to women, with her asking why those who are not gay now turn to other women instead of holding out for the right opportunity; of course she got a lot flax for it; with some of the responses being very immature and defensive. With me, myself, desiring to know, what if* *the man of your dreams did come along after making a choice like this? With me also wondering if you care how you look, the consequences you may garner, or the heartbreak you cause others from using them for temporary purposes due to loneliness (I mean really is it that serious) or curiosity; something from my point of view shows how selfish this endeavor is with it possibly being why the question was originally posed by Jada, though I can't speak for her. Another point also from this is for all those who feel ok about going this route from the feeling, that because there are no ACCEPTABLE men to date, their options are running out, with maybe the problem being your outlook on what's acceptable and not the men themselves; something again all saying that until you are right in your life, with your values being correct, you won't recognized what a good man is, leaving you vulnerability to those who want to take advantage of your current state of disillusionment, pacifying behavior that may need to be corrected.).* **Now** as this particular discussion relates to men, be careful about being too obliging to the lesbian community when it comes to assisting them with procreation, because you could find yourself being caught up in paternity issues later if things don't' work out in their relationship with you having to pay child support, a situation occurring in the state of Kansas, where the custodian parent, needing assistance, was forced to give up the name of the man whose sperm was used to impregnate her and the courts going after him, something making very little sense *(and now I'm sure he regrets ever involving himself in with him possibly incurring a burden he wasn't expecting)* from the reasoning behind why the defunct relationship existed in the first place, replacing what Yah has sanctioned as being valid with what man has now sanctioned as valid *(and what some in society finding not necessarily true from the revelation on* *the importance of having both the child's mother and father in their life*), **but hey I just had to ask . . . .**

OH YEAH P. S. You can't put race and sexuality in the same bag, because with one (*the former*) being definitely something that can't be changed (*with it being a physical issue*) where as with the latter, it is all about behavior (*or a state of mind*) which you can, SO PLEASE STOP GROUPING THE TWO AS IF THEY SHOULD BE REGARDED IN THE SAME LIGHT . . . . This has been a public service announcement, thank you very much!!!!!!!!!!!!!!!!!!!!

Made in the USA
Middletown, DE
06 October 2022

12146456R00194